From

Welcome to our extra-special astrological forecast which takes up to the end of the century on our year-ahead guides all the astrological calculations had to be made using tables and a calculator. Today, by the miracle of computers, we have been able to build our knowledge and hard work into a program which calculates the precise astrological aspect for every day in a flash.

When Shakespeare wrote 'The fault, dear Brutus, is not in our stars, but in ourselves', he spoke for every astrologer. In our day-to-day forecasts we cannot hope to be 100% accurate every time, because this would remove the most important influence in your life, which is you! What we can hope to do is to give you a sense of the astrological backdrop to the day, week or month in question, and so prompt you to think a little harder about what is going in your own life, and thus help improve your chances of acting effectively to deal with events and situations.

During the course of a year, there may be one or two readings that are similar in nature. This is not an error, it is simply that the Moon or a planet has repeated a particular pattern. In addition, a planetary pattern that applies to your sign may apply to someone else's sign at some other point during the year. One planetary 'return' that you already know well is the Solar return that occurs every year on your birthday.

If you've read our guides before, you'll know that we're never less than positive and that our advice is unpretentious, down to earth, and rooted in daily experience. If this is the first time you've met us, please regard us not as in any way astrological gurus, but as good friends who wish you nothing but health, prosperity and contentment. Happy 1998-9!

Sasha Fenton is a world-renowned astrologer, palmist and Tarot card reader, with over 80 books published on Astrology, Palmistry, Tarot and other forms of divination. Now living in London, Sasha is a regular broadcaster on radio and television, as well as making frequent contributions to newspapers and magazines around the world, including South Africa and Australia. She is a former President and Secretary of the British Astrological and Psychic Society (BAPS) and Secretary of the Advisory Panel on Astrological Education.

Jonathan Dee is an astrologer, artist and historian based in Wales, and a direct descendant of the great Elizabethan alchemist and wizard Dr John Dee, court astrologer to Queen Elizabeth I. He has written a number of books, including the recently completed *The Chronicles of Ancient Egypt,* and for the last five years has co-written an annual astrological forecast series with Sasha Fenton. A regular broadcaster on television and radio, he has also hosted the Starline show for KQED Talk Radio, New Mexico.

YOUR DAY-BY-DAY FORECAST
SEPTEMBER 1998 – DECEMBER 1999

SASHA FENTON • JONATHAN DEE

HALDANE • MASON

Zambezi

DEDICATION
For the memory of Gary Bailey, a new star in heaven.

ACKNOWLEDGEMENTS
With many thanks to our computer wizard, Sean Lovatt.

This edition published 1998
by Haldane Mason Ltd
59 Chepstow Road
London W2 5BP

Copyright © Sasha Fenton and Jonathan Dee 1998

All rights reserved. No part of this publication may be reproduced, stored in a retrieval system, or transmitted, in any form or by any means, electronic, mechanical, photocopying, recording or otherwise, without the prior permission of the publishers.

Sasha Fenton and Jonathan Dee assert the moral right to be identified as the authors of this work.

ISBN 1-902463-11-0

Designed and produced by Haldane Mason Ltd
Cover illustration by Lo Cole
Edited by Jan Budkowski

Printed in Singapore by Craft Print Pte Ltd

CONTENTS

AN ASTROLOGICAL OVERVIEW OF THE 20TH CENTURY	6
THE ESSENTIAL SCORPIO	16
YOUR SUN SIGN	20
ALL THE OTHER SUN SIGNS	21
YOU AND YOURS	29
YOUR RISING SIGN	36
SCORPIO IN LOVE	41
YOUR PROSPECTS FOR 1999	43
SCORPIO IN THE FINAL QUARTER OF 1998	46
SCORPIO IN 1999	69

SCORPIO

An Astrological Overview of the 20th Century

Next year the shops will be full of astrology books for the new century and also for the new millennium. In this book, the last of the old century, we take a brief look back to see where the slow-moving outer planets were in each decade and what it meant. Obviously this will be no more than a very brief glance backwards but next year you will be able to see the picture in much more depth when we bring out our own book for the new millennium.

1900 - 1909
The century began with Pluto in Gemini and it was still in Gemini by the end of the decade. Neptune started out in Gemini but moved into cancer in 1901 and ended the decade still in Cancer. Uranus started the century in Sagittarius, moving to Capricorn in 1904 and ending the decade still in Capricorn. Saturn began the century in Sagittarius, moving to Capricorn in January 1900 and then through Aquarius, Pisces and Aries, ending the decade in Aries.

The stars and the decade
In general terms, the planet of upheaval in the dynastic sign of Sagittarius with Saturn also in that sign and Pluto opposing it, all at the very start of the century put the spotlight on dynasties, royalty and empires. As Saturn left for the 'establishment' sign of Capricorn these just about held together but as the decade ended, the power and control that these ancient dynasties had were loosening their grip on the developed world of the time. Queen Victoria died in 1901 and her son, Edward VII was dying by the end of the decade, so in Britain, the Victorian age of certainty was already coming to an end. The Boer War was only just won by Britain in 1902 which brought a shock to this successful colonial country.

Pluto in Gemini brought a transformation in methods of communications. It was as Saturn entered the innovative sign of Aquarius that these took concrete and useful form. Thus it was during this decade that the motor car, telephone, typewriter, gramophone and colour photography came into existence. Air travel began in 1900 with the first Zeppelin airship flight, the first powered aeroplane flight by the Wright brothers in 1904 and Louis Blériot's flight across the English Channel in 1909. Edison demonstrated the Kinetophone, the first machine capable of showing talking moving pictures in

1910. Even the nature of war changed as technologically modern Japan managed to fight off the might of the Russian empire in the war of 1904 - 1905.

The Treaty of Versailles, followed by further treaties of Aix and Trianon served to crush the German nation and therefore sow the seeds of the next war.

1910 - 1919

Pluto opened the decade in Gemini, moving to Cancer in 1913. Neptune travelled from Cancer to Leo in September 1914 while Uranus moved out of Capricorn, through Aquarius to end the decade in Pisces. Saturn moved from Aries to Taurus, then to Gemini, back into Taurus, then into Gemini again entering Cancer in 1914, then on through Leo and ending the decade in Virgo.

The stars and the decade

Now we see the start of a pattern. Sagittarius may be associated with dynasties but it is the home-loving and patriotic signs of Cancer and Leo that actually seem to be associated with major wars. The desire either to expand a country's domestic horizons or to protect them from the expansion of others is ruled by the maternal sign of Cancer, followed by the paternal one of Leo. Home, family, tradition, safety all seem to be fought over when major planets move through these signs. When future generations learn about the major wars of the 20th century they will probably be lumped together in their minds - despite the 20-year gap between them - just as we lump the Napoleonic wars together, forgetting that there was a nine-year gap between them, and of course, this long stay of Pluto in Cancer covered the whole of this period.

It is interesting to note that Pluto moved into Cancer in July 1913 and Neptune entered Leo on the 23rd of September 1914, just three of weeks after the outbreak of the First World War. Saturn moved into Cancer in April 1914. Pluto is associated with transformation, Neptune with dissolution and Saturn with loss, sadness and sickness. Many people suffered and so many families and dynasties were unexpectedly dissolved at that time, among these, the Romanov Czar and his family and the kings of Portugal, Hungary, Italy and Germany and the Manchu dynasty of China. America (born on the 4th of July, 1776 and therefore a Cancerian country) was thrust into prominence as a major economic and social power after this war. Russia experienced the Bolshevik revolution during it. As Saturn moved into Virgo (the sign that is associated with health) at the end of this decade, a world-wide plague of influenza killed 20 million people, far more than had died during the course of the war itself.

SCORPIO

1920 - 1929

The roaring 20s began and ended with Pluto in Cancer. Neptune moved from Leo to Virgo at the end of this decade and Uranus moved from Pisces to Aries in 1927. Saturn travelled from Virgo, through Libra, Scorpio, Sagittarius and then backwards and forwards between Sagittarius and Capricorn, ending up in Capricorn at the end of 1929.

The stars and the decade

Pluto's long transformative reign in Cancer made life hard for men during this time. Cancer is the most female of all the signs, being associated with nurturing and motherhood. Many men were sick in mind and body as a result of the war and women began to take proper jobs for the first time. Family planning and better living conditions brought improvements in life for ordinary people and in the developed world there was a major boom in house building as well as in improved road and rail commuter systems. The time of lords and ladies was passing and ordinary people were demanding better conditions. Strikes and unrest were common, especially in Germany. As the decade ended, the situation both domestically and in the foreign policies of the developed countries began to look up. Even the underdeveloped countries began to modernize a little. Shortly before the middle of this decade, all the politicians who might have prevented the rise of Hitler and the Nazi party died and then came the stock market crash of 1929. The probable astrological sequence that set this train of circumstances off was the run up to the opposition of Saturn in Capricorn to Pluto in Cancer which took place in 1931. The effects of such major planetary events are often felt while the planets are closing into a conjunction or opposition etc., rather than just at the time of their exactitude.

On a brighter note great strides were made in the worlds of art, music and film and ordinary people could enjoy more entertainment than ever before, in 1929 the first colour television was demonstrated and in 1928 Alexander Fleming announced his discovery of penicillin. At the very start of the decade prohibition passed into US Federal law, ushering in the age of organized crime and as a spin-off a great increase in drinking in that country and later on, all those wonderful gangster films. The same year, the partition of Ireland took place bringing more conflict and this time on a very long-term basis.

1930 - 1939

The 1930s should have been better than the 1920s but they were not. Pluto remained in Cancer until 1937, Neptune remained in Virgo throughout the decade, Uranus entered Taurus in 1934 and Saturn moved from Capricorn

SCORPIO

through Aquarius, Pisces then back and forth between Aries and Pisces, ending the decade in Taurus.

The stars and the decade

Neptune's voyage through Virgo did help in the field of advances in medicine and in public health. Pluto continued to make life hard for men and then by extension for families, while in the 'motherhood' sign of Cancer. While Saturn was in the governmental signs of Capricorn and Aquarius, democracy ceased to exist anywhere in the world. In the UK a coalition government was in power for most of the decade while in the USA, Franklin Delano Roosevelt ruled as a kind of benign emperor for almost three terms of office, temporarily dismantling much of that country's democratic machinery while he did so. Governments in Russia, Germany, Italy, Spain and Japan moved to dictatorships or dictatorial types of government with all the resultant tyranny, while France, Britain and even the USA floundered for much of the time. China was ruled by warring factions. However, there was an upsurge of popular entertainment at this time, especially through the mediums of film, music and radio probably due to the advent of adventurous, inventive Uranus into the music and entertainment sign of Taurus in 1934.

1940 - 1949

War years once again. Pluto remained in the 'paternal' sign of Leo throughout this decade, bringing tyranny and control of the masses in all the developed countries and also much of the Third World. Neptune entered Libra in 1942, Uranus moved from Taurus to Gemini in 1941, then to Cancer in 1948. Saturn began the decade in Taurus, moved to Gemini, Cancer, Leo and finally Virgo during this decade. The 'home and country' signs of Cancer and Leo were once more thrust into the limelight in a war context. Neptune is not a particularly warlike planet and Libra is normally a peaceable sign but Libra does rule open enemies as well as peace and harmony.

The stars and the decade

To continue looking for the moment at the planet Neptune, astrologers don't take its dangerous side seriously enough. Neptune can use the sea in a particularly destructive manner when it wants to with tidal waves, disasters at sea and so on, so it is interesting to note that the war in the West was almost lost for the allies at sea due to the success of the German U-boats. Hitler gambled on a quick end to the war in the east and shut his mind to Napoleon's experience of the Russian winter. Saturn through Cancer and Leo, followed by the inventive sign of Uranus entering Cancer at the end of

SCORPIO

the decade almost brought home, family, tradition and the world itself to an end with the explosions of the first atomic bombs.

However, towards the end of this decade, it became clear that democracy, the rights of ordinary people and a better lifestyle for everybody were a better answer than trying to find 'lebensraum' by pinching one's neighbour's land and enslaving its population. Saturn's entry into Virgo brought great advances in medicine and the plagues and diseases of the past began to diminish throughout the world. Pluto in Leo transformed the power structures of every country and brought such ideas as universal education, better housing and social security systems - at least in the developed world.

1950 - 1959

Pluto still dipped in and out of Leo until it finally left for Virgo in 1957. Neptune finally left Libra for Scorpio in 1955, Uranus sat on that dangerous and warlike cusp of Cancer and Leo, while Saturn moved swiftly through Virgo, Libra, Scorpio, Sagittarius and then into Capricorn.

The stars and the decade

The confrontations between dictators and between dictatorships and democracy continued during this time with the emphasis shifting to the conflict between communism and capitalism. The Korean war started the decade and the communist take-over in China ended it. Military alertness was reflected in the UK by the two years of national service that young men were obliged to perform throughout the decade. Rationing, shortages of food, fuel and consumer goods remained in place for half the decade, but by the end of it, the world was becoming a very different place. With American money, Germany and Japan were slowly rebuilt, communism did at least bring a measure of stability in China and the Soviet Union, although its pervasive power brought fear and peculiar witch hunts in the United States. In Europe and the USA the lives of ordinary people improved beyond belief.

Pluto in Virgo brought plenty of work for the masses and for ordinary people, poverty began to recede for the first time in history. Better homes, labour-saving devices and the vast amount of popular entertainment in the cinema, the arts, popular music and television at long last brought fun into the lives of most ordinary folk. In Britain and the Commonwealth, in June 1953, the coronation of the new Queen ushered in a far more optimistic age while her Empire dissolved around her.

SCORPIO

1960 - 1969

This is the decade that today's middle-aged folk look back on with fond memories, yet it was not always as safe as we like to think. Pluto remained in Virgo throughout the decade bringing work and better health to many people. Neptune remained in Scorpio throughout this time, while Uranus traversed back and forth between Leo and Virgo, then from Virgo to Libra, ending the decade in Libra. Saturn hovered around the cusp of Taurus and Gemini until the middle of the decade and then on through Gemini and Cancer, spending time around the Cancer/Leo cusp and then on through Leo to rest once again on the Leo/Virgo cusp.

The stars and the decade

The Cancer/Leo threats of atomic war were very real in the early 1960s, with the Cuban missile crisis bringing America and the Soviet Union to the point of war. The Berlin wall went up. President Kennedy's assassination in November 1963 shocked the world and the atmosphere of secrets, spies and mistrust abounded in Europe, the USA and in the Soviet Union. One of the better manifestations of this time of cold war, CIA dirty tricks and spies was the plethora of wonderful spy films and television programmes of the early 60s. Another was the sheer fun of the Profumo affair!

The late 1960s brought the start of a very different atmosphere. The Vietnam War began to be challenged by the teenagers whose job it was to die in it and the might of America was severely challenged by these tiny Vietcong soldiers in black pyjamas and sandals. The wave of materialism of the 1950s was less attractive to the flower-power generation of the late 60s. The revolutionary planet Uranus in balanced Libra brought the protest movement into being and an eventual end to racial segregation in the USA. Equality between the sexes was beginning to be considered. The troubles of Northern Ireland began at the end of this decade.

In 1969, Neil Armstrong stepped out onto the surface of the Moon, thereby marking the start of a very different age, the New Age, the Age of Aquarius.

1970 - 1979

Pluto began the decade around the Virgo/Libra cusp, settling in Libra in 1972 and remaining there for the rest of the decade. Neptune started the decade by moving back and forth between Scorpio and Sagittarius and residing in Sagittarius for the rest of the decade. Uranus hovered between Libra and Scorpio until 1975 and then travelled through Scorpio until the end of the decade while Saturn moved from Taurus to Gemini, then hung around the Cancer/Leo cusp and finally moved into Virgo.

SCORPIO

The stars and the decade

The planets in or around that dangerous Cancer/Leo cusp and the continuing Libran emphasis brought more danger from total war as America struggled with Vietnam and the cold war. However, the influence of Virgo brought work, an easier life and more hope than ever to ordinary people in the First World. Uranus in Libra brought different kinds of love partnerships into public eye as fewer people bothered to marry. Divorce became easier and homosexuality became legal. With Uranus opening the doors to secretive Scorpio, spies such as Burgess, Maclean, Philby, Lonsdale and Penkowski began to come in from the cold. President Nixon was nicely caught out at Watergate, ushering in a time of more openness in governments everywhere.

If you are reading this book, you may be doing so because you are keen to know about yourself and your sign, but you are likely to be quite interested in astrology and perhaps in other esoteric techniques. You can thank the atmosphere of the 1970s for the openness and the lack of fear and superstition which these subjects now enjoy. The first festival of Mind, Body and Spirit took place in 1976 and the British Astrological and Psychic Society was launched in the same year, both of these events being part of the increasing interest in personal awareness and alternative lifestyles.

Neptune in Scorpio brought fuel crises and Saturn through Cancer and Leo brought much of the repression of women to an end, with some emancipation from tax and social anomalies. Tea bags and instant coffee allowed men for the first time to cope with the terrible hardship of making a cuppa!

1980 - 1989

Late in 1983, Pluto popped into the sign of Scorpio, popped out again and re-entered it in 1984. Astrologers of the 60s and 70s feared this planetary situation in case it brought the ultimate Plutonic destruction with it. Instead of this, the Soviet Union and South Africa freed themselves from tyranny and the Berlin Wall came down. The main legacy of Pluto in Scorpio is the Scorpionic association of danger through sex, hence the rise of AIDS. Neptune began the decade in Sagittarius then it travelled back and forth over the Sagittarius/Capricorn cusp, ending the decade in Capricorn. Uranus moved from Scorpio, back and forth over the Scorpio/Sagittarius cusp, then through Sagittarius, ending the decade in Capricorn. Saturn began the decade in Virgo, then hovered around the Virgo/Libra cusp, through Libra, Scorpio and Sagittarius, resting along the Sagittarius/Capricorn cusp, ending the decade in Capricorn.

SCORPIO

The stars and the decade

The movement of planets through the dynastic sign of Sagittarius brought doubt and uncertainty to Britain's royal family, while the planets in authoritative Capricorn brought strong government to the UK in the form of Margaret Thatcher. Ordinary people began to seriously question the *status quo* and to attempt to change it. Even in the hidden empire of China, modernization and change began to creep in. Britain went to war again by sending the gunboats to the Falkland Islands to fight off a truly old-fashioned takeover bid by the daft Argentinean dictator, General Galtieri.

Saturn is an earth planet, Neptune rules the sea, while Uranus is associated with the air. None of these planets was in their own element and this may have had something to do with the increasing number of natural and man-made disasters that disrupted the surface of the earth during this decade. The first space shuttle flight took place in 1981 and the remainder of the decade reflected many people's interest in extra-terrestrial life in the form of films and television programmes. ET went home. Black rap music and the casual use of drugs became a normal part of the youth scene. Maybe the movement of escapist Neptune through the 'outer space' sign of Sagittarius had something to do with this.

1990 - 1999

Pluto began the decade in Scorpio, moving in and out of Sagittarius until 1995 remaining there for the rest of the decade. Neptune began the decade in Capricorn, travelling back and forth over the cusp of Aquarius, ending the decade in Aquarius. Uranus moved in and out of Aquarius, remaining there from 1996 onwards. Saturn travelled from Capricorn, through Aquarius, Pisces (and back again), then on through Pisces, Aries, in and out of Taurus, finally ending the decade in Taurus.

The stars and the decade

The Aquarian emphasis has brought advances in science and technology and a time when computers are common even in the depths of darkest Africa. The logic and fairness of Aquarius does seem to have affected many of the peoples of the earth. Pluto in the open sign of Sagittarius brought much governmental secrecy to an end, it will also transform the traditional dynasties of many countries before it leaves them for good. The aftermath of the dreadful and tragic death of Princess Diana in 1997 put a rocket under the creaking 19th-century habits of British royalty.

The final decade began with yet another war – this time the Gulf War – which sent a serious signal to all those who fancy trying their hand at international bullying or the 19th-century tactics of pinching your neighbour's land and resources. Uranus's last fling in Capricorn tore up the earth with volcanoes and earthquakes, and its stay in Aquarius seems to be keeping this pattern going. Saturn in Pisces, opposite the 'health' sign of Virgo is happily bringing new killer viruses into being and encouraging old ones to build up resistance to antibiotics. The bubonic plague is alive and well in tropical countries along with plenty of other plagues that either are, or are becoming resistant to modern medicines. Oddly enough the planetary line-up in 1997 was similar to that of the time of the great plague of London in 1665!

Films, the arts, architecture all showed signs of beginning an exciting period of revolution in 1998. Life became more electronic and computer-based for the younger generation while in the old world, the vast army of the elderly began to struggle with a far less certain world of old-age poverty and strange and frightening innovations. Keeping up to date and learning to adapt is the only way to survive now, even for the old folks.

It is interesting to note that the first event of importance to shock Europe in this century was the morganatic marriage of Franz Ferdinand, the heir to the massively powerful Austro-Hungarian throne. This took place in the summer of 1900. The unpopularity of this controlling and repressive empire fell on its head in Sarajevo on the 28th of July 1914. This mighty empire is now almost forgotten, but its death throes are still being played out in and around Sarajevo today - which only goes to show how long it can take for anything to be settled.

Technically the twentieth century only ends at the beginning of the year 2001 but most of us will be celebrating the end of the century and the end of the millennium and the end of the last day of 1999 - that is if we are all here of course! A famous prediction of global disaster comes from the writings of the French writer, doctor and astrologer Nostradamus (1503–66):

- The year 1999, seventh month,
- From the sky will come a great King of Terror:
- To bring back to life the great King of the Mongols,
- Before and after Mars reigns.
  (Quatrain X:72 from the *Centuries*)

Jonathan has worked out that with the adjustments of the calendar from the time of Nostradamus, the date of the predicted disaster will be the 11th of August 1999. As it happens there will be a total eclipse of the Sun at ten past eleven on that day at 18 degrees of Leo. We have already seen how the signs of Cancer, Leo and Libra seem to be the ones that are most clearly associated with war and this reference to 'Mars reigning' is the fact that Mars is the god of war. Therefore, the prediction suggests that an Oriental king will wage a war from the sky that brings terror to the world. Some people have suggested that this event would bring about the end of the world but that is not what the prediction actually says. A look back over the 1900s has proved this whole century to be one of terror from the skies but it would be awful to think that there would be yet another war, this time emanating from Mongolia. Terrible but not altogether impossible to imagine I guess. Well, let us hope that we are all here for us to write and for you to enjoy the next set of zodiac books for the turn of the millennium and beyond.

2000 onwards: a very brief look forward

The scientific exploration and eventual colonization of space is on the way now. Scorpio rules fossil fuels and there will be no major planets passing through this sign for quite a while so alternative fuel sources will have to be sought. Maybe it will be the entry of Uranus into the pioneering sign of Aries in January 2012 that will make a start on this. The unusual line up of the 'ancient seven' planets of Sun, Moon, Mercury, Venus, Mars and Saturn in Taurus on the 5th of May 2000 will be interesting. Taurus represents such matters as land, farming, building, cooking, flowers, the sensual beauty of music, dancing and the arts. Jonathan and Sasha will work out the astrological possibilities for the future in depth and put out ideas together for you in a future book.

SCORPIO

The Essential Scorpio

YOUR RULING PLANET Your ruling body is Pluto, the Roman god of the underworld. Pluto is associated with great wealth, most of which is hidden underground, as well as birth, death and sex. Before Pluto was discovered, Scorpio was assigned to Mars, the red planet, which is associated with the Roman god of war.

YOUR SYMBOL The scorpion is your symbol. The scorpion once made the mistake of stinging the giant, Orion, who threw him into the sky where he now exists as far as away from Orion as is possible. The scorpion turns its sting on itself if it feels threatened. The ancient symbol for your sign used to be the eagle. This denotes the higher side of Scorpio, which can soar above everything that is base, coarse and petty.

PARTS OF THE BODY The sexual organs, the lower stomach, lower spine and groin. Also blood and eyes.

YOUR GOOD BITS You have great endurance, tenacity and self-control. Your willpower will overcome almost anything. You are very caring and protective towards your family, especially your partner.

YOUR BAD BITS You can be secretive, suspicious, inflexible, vindictive and ruthless.

YOUR WEAKNESSES Self-destruction, violence, moodiness, clannishness.

YOUR BEST DAY Tuesday. Tuesday is traditionally assigned to the Roman god, Mars.

YOUR WORST DAY Friday.

YOUR COLOURS Dark red, dark purple.

CITIES Milwaukee, Washington DC, New Orleans, Liverpool, Brisbane.

COUNTRIES Norway, Syria, Brazil, Zimbabwe.

SCORPIO

HOLIDAYS You are too restless to sit about on a beach for long. A sea cruise probably appeals because you love the sea and you enjoy waking up in new places every day.

YOUR FAVOURITE CAR You need a big, fast, powerful automatic limo with tinted windows and plenty of gadgets in it. An ejector seat for irritating passengers would be nice.

YOUR FAVOURITE MEAL OUT Your stomach is sensitive, so spicy foods and anything that is unfamiliar is not liked. Many Scorpios enjoy eating soup, either the thin kind with a little pasta added or a thick country broth. Traditional astrology suggests peppers; we suggest that you hold the peppers and go for the leeks instead!

YOUR FAVOURITE DRINK Scorpios either drink a great deal or practically nothing at all. Many of you enjoy whisky, especially the many different kinds of malts.

YOUR HERB Basil.

YOUR TREES Blackthorn, hawthorn, or any thorny bush or tree, possibly something like acacia.

YOUR FLOWERS Rhododendron, dark red flowers, also cacti.

YOUR ANIMALS Scorpion, eagle, shark, mule and snake.

YOUR METAL Iron. This metal is associated with Mars, the ancient ruler of Scorpio. Iron has a low melting point and it oxidizes, or rusts, to a reddish colour. These days plutonium has been added as a Scorpio metal, but it isn't recommended to wear this as jewellery!

YOUR GEMS Opal, obsidian, onyx, jet, marcasite.

MODE OF DRESS You love to shock, so you could turn up looking like Cher in one of her more outrageous outfits. Otherwise, both sexes like wearing casual clothes such as jeans and colourful shirts.

YOUR CAREERS Police, forensic or medical work, especially surgery and psychiatry. Butcher, miner, engineer.

SCORPIO

YOUR FRIENDS People who are not afraid of you and who are as passionate about life as you are.

YOUR ENEMIES Timid types or aloof, pretentious ones.

YOUR FAVOURITE GIFTS You hate anything that is cheap and nasty so any gift, however small, should be of the highest quality. You love music so a couple of CDs or tickets to a musical or pop event would delight you. Nice clothes or something attractive for the home always goes down well, as does aftershave, perfume or good jewellery. Sports or photographic equipment is also liked.

YOUR IDEAL HOME Whatever the home you have, you prefer to have the mortgage paid off! A large house with plenty of land appeals as you hate being confined to a flat or overlooked by others. You would probably love to have a study of your own where you can keep your collection of old bills and other bits of paper under lock and key and where you can chat on the phone without being overheard.

YOUR FAVOURITE BOOKS Factual and history books, especially about wars and exciting times. Also war and spy stories, thrillers and novels with an occult theme.

YOUR FAVOURITE MUSIC Classical, some pop, also country and western music.

YOUR GAMES AND SPORTS Rugby, rough team games, swimming, potholing, boxing, sword-play, archery, fishing. In short, anything where you can really stretch your body and bludgeon others!

YOUR PAST AND FUTURE LIVES There are many theories about past lives and even some about future ones, but we suggest that your immediate past life was ruled by the sign previous to Scorpio and that your future life will be governed by the sign that follows Scorpio. Therefore you were Libra in your previous life and will be Sagittarius in the next. If you want to know all about either of these signs, zip straight out to the shops and buy our books on them!

YOUR LUCKY NUMBER Your lucky number is 8. To find your lucky number on a raffle ticket or something similar, first add the numbers

SCORPIO

together. For example, if one of your lottery numbers is 28, add 2 + 8 to make 10; then add 1 + 0, to give the root number of 1. The number 316 on a raffle ticket works in the same way. Add 3 + 1 + 6 to make 10: then add 1 + 0, making 1. As any number that adds up to 8 is lucky for you, numbers 17, 161 or 314 would work. A selection of lottery numbers should include some of the following: 8, 17, 26, 35 or 44.

SCORPIO

Your Sun Sign

*Your Sun Sign is determined by your date of birth.
Thus anyone born between 21st March and 20th April is Aries and so
on through the calendar. Your Rising Sign (see page 36)
is determined by the day and time of your birth.*

SCORPIO

RULED BY PLUTO AND MARS
24th October to 22nd November

Yours is a feminine, water sign whose symbol is the scorpion. The feminine, water aspect suggests that yours is a gentle and loving sign, yet Scorpios have a very bad press in all astrology books, being described as passionate, determined, hot-tempered, drunken, cruel and vengeful. The truth, as you shall see, is somewhere in between.

You have the greatest endurance of any sign of the zodiac. You can cope with a hard job, a difficult partner or a set of crushing circumstances better than most. You have great pride and very high personal standards and you would consider yourself spineless if you walked away from trouble. You are extremely loyal and very loving to those whom you are close to. You don't let your family down and you can even care for a cantankerous parent if necessary. However, you don't keep your feelings to yourself and, if you are being put upon, you let people know it. The one thing you really cannot take is being abandoned or betrayed by someone in whom you have placed your trust, and you don't forgive anyone who parts you from anything or anyone you consider to be yours.

Something in your childhood may have undermined your confidence. Your parents may have preferred another sister or brother to you, or you may have been made to feel inferior or insecure by schoolmates, or by the people whom you lived amongst. You could, alternatively, have been envied by others for being brighter than them. You are slow to trust others, and you don't let other people into the secrets of your bank account, your private life or your real feelings. Only those who love you know when all isn't well, because you don't allow others to see what you deem to be weakness or failure. Some of you feel that you are missing out on your share of money, love or other goodies. When a situation becomes intolerable, either in personal life or in a job, you can set about destroying it completely, cutting your own nose off

SCORPIO

to spite your face in the process. If you manage to find the right partner and the right boss, you are the soul of loyalty and you will do all that you can for them. You will support your partner in his or her career and you would sacrifice anything in order to push a talented child. This scenario does not fit all Scorpios because there are plenty of you who have happy childhoods and good relationships in adult life. However, you may be drawn to choose a difficult partner who presents a challenge.

Some of you are as sexy as your reputation says you are, while others go through life being surprisingly innocent and inhibited. All of you enjoy being thought of as sexy and some of you enjoy making saucy remarks. You are honest, dependable, talented and, when you want to be, extremely charming. You probably have a wonderful speaking voice and a sharp intellect. People either love you dearly or fear you. You can be terribly afraid of life itself at times and you can worry yourself sick about practically anything, but you have the courage and endurance to overcome almost anything. You have the most wonderful recuperative powers and can overcome even death itself – for a while at least.

All the Other Sun Signs

ARIES
21st March to 20th April

Ariens can get anything they want off the ground, but they may land back down again with a bump. Quick to think and to act, Ariens are often intelligent and have little patience with fools. This includes anyone who is slower than themselves.

They are not the tidiest of people and they are impatient with details, except when engaged upon their special subject; then Ariens can fiddle around for hours. They are willing to make huge financial sacrifices for their families and they can put up with relatives living with them as long as this leaves them free to do their own thing. Aries women are decisive and competitive at work but many are disinterested in homemaking. They might consider giving up a relationship if it interfered with their ambitions. Highly sexed and experimental, they are faithful while in love but, if love begins to fade, they start to look around. Ariens may tell themselves that they are only looking for amusement, but they may end up in a fulfilling relationship with someone else's partner. This kind of situation offers the continuity and emotional support

SCORPIO

which they need with no danger of boredom or entrapment.

Their faults are those of impatience and impetuosity, coupled with a hot temper. They can pick a furious row with a supposed adversary, tear him or her to pieces then walk away from the situation five minutes later, forgetting all about it. Unfortunately, the poor victim can't always shake off the effects of the row in quite the same way. However, Arien cheerfulness, spontaneous generosity and kindness make them the greatest friends to have.

TAURUS
21st April to 21st May

These people are practical and persevering. Taureans are solid and reliable, regular in habits, sometimes a bit wet behind the ears and stubborn as mules. Their love of money and the comfort it can bring may make them very materialistic in outlook. They are most suited to a practical career which brings with it few surprises and plenty of money. However, they have a strong artistic streak which can be expressed in work, hobbies and interests.

Some Taureans are quick and clever, highly amusing and quite outrageous in appearance, but underneath this crazy exterior is a background of true talent and very hard work. This type may be a touch arrogant. Other Taureans hate to be rushed or hassled, preferring to work quietly and thoroughly at their own pace. They take relationships very seriously and make safe and reliable partners. They may keep their worries to themselves but they are not usually liars or sexually untrustworthy.

Being so very sensual as well as patient, these people make excellent lovers. Their biggest downfall comes later in life when they have a tendency to plonk themselves down in front of the television night after night, tuning out the rest of the world. Another problem with some Taureans is their 'pet hate', which they'll harp on about at any given opportunity. Their virtues are common sense, loyalty, responsibility and a pleasant, non-hostile approach to others. Taureans are much brighter than anyone gives them credit, and it is hard to beat them in an argument because they usually know what they are talking about. If a Taurean is on your side, they make wonderful friends and comfortable and capable colleagues.

GEMINI
22nd May to 21st June

Geminis are often accused of being short on intellect and unable to stick to anyone or anything for long. In a nutshell, great fun at a party but totally unreliable. This is unfair: nobody works harder, is more reliable or capable than Geminis when they put their mind to a task, especially if there is a chance of making large sums of money! Unfortunately, they have a low boredom threshold and they can drift away from something or someone when it no longer interests them. They like to be busy, with plenty of variety in their lives and the opportunity to communicate with others. Their forte lies in the communications industry where they shamelessly pinch ideas and improve on them. Many Geminis are highly ambitious people who won't allow anything or anyone to stand in their way.

They are surprisingly constant in relationships, often marrying for life but, if it doesn't work out, they will walk out and put the experience behind them. Geminis need relationships and if one fails, they will soon start looking for the next. Faithfulness is another story, however, because the famous Gemini curiosity can lead to any number of adventures. Geminis educate their children well while neglecting to see whether they have a clean shirt. The house is full of books, videos, televisions, CDs, newspapers and magazines and there is a phone in every room as well as in the car, the loo and the Gemini lady's handbag.

CANCER
22nd June to 23rd July

Cancerians look for security on the one hand and adventure and novelty on the other. They are popular because they really listen to what others are saying. Their own voices are attractive too. They are naturals for sales work and in any kind of advisory capacity. Where their own problems are concerned, they can disappear inside themselves and brood, which makes it hard for others to understand them. Cancerians spend a good deal of time worrying about their families and, even more so, about money. They appear soft but are very hard to influence.

Many Cancerians are small traders and many more work in teaching or the caring professions. They have a feel for history, perhaps collecting historical mementoes, and their memories are excellent. They need to have a home but they love to travel away from it, being happy in the knowledge that it is there waiting for them to come back to. There are a few Cancerians who seem to drift through life and expect other members of their family to keep them.

Romantically, they prefer to be settled and they fear being alone. A marriage would need to be really bad before they consider leaving, and if they do, they soon look for a new partner. These people can be scoundrels in business because they hate parting with money once they have their hands on it. However, their charm and intelligence usually manage to get them out of trouble.

LEO
24th July to 23rd August

Leos can be marvellous company or a complete pain in the neck. Under normal circumstances, they are warm-hearted, generous, sociable and popular but they can be very moody and irritable when under pressure or under the weather. Leos put their heart and soul into whatever they are doing and they can work like demons for a while. However, they cannot keep up the pace for long and they need to get away, zonk out on the sofa and take frequent holidays. These people always appear confident and they look like true winners, but their confidence can suddenly evaporate, leaving them unsure and unhappy with their efforts. They are extremely sensitive to hurt and they cannot take ridicule or even very much teasing.

Leos are proud. They have very high standards in all that they do and most have great integrity and honesty, but there are some who are complete and utter crooks. These people can stand on their dignity and be very snobbish. Their arrogance can become insufferable and they can take their powers of leadership into the realms of bossiness. They are convinced that they should be in charge and they can be very obstinate. Some Leos love the status and lifestyle which proclaims their successes. Many work in glamour professions such as the airline and entertainment industries. Others spend their day communing with computers and other high-tech gadgetry. In loving relationships, they are loyal but only while the magic lasts. If boredom sets in, they often start looking around for fresh fields. They are the most generous and loving of people and they need to play affectionately. Leos are kind, charming and they live life to the full.

VIRGO
24th August to 23rd September

Virgos are highly intelligent, interested in everything and everyone and happy to be busy with many jobs and hobbies. Many have some kind of specialized knowledge and most are good with their hands, but their nit-picking ways can infuriate colleagues. They find it hard to discuss their innermost feelings and this can make them hard to understand. In many ways, they are happier doing something practical than dealing with relationships. Virgos can also overdo the self-sacrificial bit and make themselves martyrs to other people's impractical lifestyles. They are willing to fit in with whatever is going on and can adjust to most things, but they mustn't neglect their own needs.

Although excellent communicators and wonderfully witty conversationalists, Virgos prefer to express their deepest feelings by actions rather than words. Most avoid touching all but very close friends and family members and many find lovey-dovey behaviour embarrassing. They can be very highly sexed and may use this as a way of expressing love. Virgos are criticized a good deal as children and are often made to feel unwelcome in their childhood homes. In turn, they become very critical of others and they can use this in order to wound.

Many Virgos overcome inhibitions by taking up acting, music, cookery or sports. Acting is particularly common to this sign because it allows them to put aside their fears and take on the mantle of someone quite different. They are shy and slow to make friends but when they do accept someone, they are the loyalest, gentlest and kindest of companions. They are great company and have a wonderful sense of humour.

LIBRA
24th September to 23rd October

Librans have a deceptive appearance, looking soft but being tough and quite selfish underneath. Astrological tradition tells us that this sign is dedicated to marriage, but a high proportion of them prefer to remain single, particularly when a difficult relationship comes to an end. These people are great to tell secrets to because they never listen to anything properly and promptly forget whatever is said. The confusion between their desire to co-operate with others and the need for self-expression is even more evident when at work. The best job is one where they are a part of an organization but able to take responsibility and make their own decisions.

While some Librans are shy and lacking in confidence, others are strong and determined with definite leadership qualities. All need to find a job that entails dealing with others and which does not wear out their delicate nerves. All Librans are charming, sophisticated and diplomatic, but can be confusing for others. All have a strong sense of justice and fair play but most haven't the strength to take on a determinedly lame duck. They project an image which is attractive, chosen to represent their sense of status and refinement. Being inclined to experiment sexually, they are not the most faithful of partners and even goody-goody Librans are terrible flirts.

SAGITTARIUS
23rd November to 21st December

Sagittarians are great company because they are interested in everything and everyone. Broad-minded and lacking in prejudice, they are fascinated by even the strangest of people. With their optimism and humour, they are often the life and soul of the party, while they are in a good mood. They can become quite down-hearted, crabby and awkward on occasion, but not usually for long. They can be hurtful to others because they cannot resist speaking what they see as the truth, even if it causes embarrassment. However, their tactlessness is usually innocent and they have no desire to hurt.

Sagittarians need an unconventional lifestyle, preferably one which allows them to travel. They cannot be cooped up in a cramped environment and they need to meet new people and to explore a variety of ideas during their day's work. Money is not their god and they will work for a pittance if they feel inspired by the task. Their values are spiritual rather than material. Many are attracted to the spiritual side of life and may be interested in the Church, philosophy, astrology and other New Age subjects. Higher education and legal matters attract them because these subjects expand and explore intellectual boundaries. Long-lived relationships may not appeal because they need to feel free and unfettered, but they can do well with a self-sufficient and independent partner. Despite all this intellectualism and need for freedom, Sagittarians have a deep need to be cuddled and touched and they need to be supported emotionally.

CAPRICORN
22nd December to 20th January

Capricorns are patient, realistic and responsible and they take life seriously. They need security but they may find this difficult to achieve. Many live on a treadmill of work, simply to pay the bills and feed the kids. They will never shun family responsibilities, even caring for distant relatives if this becomes necessary. However, they can play the martyr while doing so. These people hate coarseness, they are easily embarrassed and they hate to annoy anyone. Capricorns believe fervently in keeping the peace in their families. This doesn't mean that they cannot stand up for themselves, indeed they know how to get their own way and they won't be bullied. They are adept at using charm to get around prickly people.

Capricorns are ambitious, hard-working, patient and status-conscious and they will work their way steadily towards the top in any organization. If they run their own businesses, they need a partner with more pizzazz to deal with sales and marketing for them while they keep an eye on the books. Their nit-picking habits can infuriate others and some have a tendency to 'know best' and not to listen. These people work at their hobbies with the same kind of dedication that they put into everything else. They are faithful and reliable in relationships and it takes a great deal to make them stray. If a relationship breaks up, they take a long time to get over it. They may marry very early or delay it until middle age when they are less shy. As an earth sign, Capricorns are highly sexed but they need to be in a relationship where they can relax and gain confidence. Their best attribute is their genuine kindness and their wonderfully dry, witty sense of humour.

AQUARIUS
21st January to 19th February

Clever, friendly, kind and humane, Aquarians are the easiest people to make friends with but probably the hardest to really know. They are often more comfortable with acquaintances than with those who are close to them. Being dutiful, they would never let a member of their family go without their basic requirements, but they can be strangely, even deliberately, blind to their underlying needs and real feelings. They are more comfortable with causes and their idealistic ideas than with the day-to-day routine of family life. Their homes may reflect this lack of interest by being rather messy, although there are other Aquarians who are almost clinically house proud.

Their opinions are formed early in life and are firmly fixed. Being patient with people, they make good teachers and are, themselves, always willing to learn something new. But are they willing to go out and earn a living? Some are, many are not. These people can be extremely eccentric in the way they dress or the way they live. They make a point of being 'different' and they can actually feel very unsettled and uneasy if made to conform, even outwardly. Their restless, sceptical minds mean that they need an alternative kind of lifestyle which stretches them mentally.

In relationships, they are surprisingly constant and faithful and they only stray when they know in their hearts that there is no longer anything to be gained from staying put. Aquarians are often very attached to the first real commitment in their lives and they can even remarry a previously divorced partner. Their sexuality fluctuates, perhaps peaking for some years then pushed aside while something else occupies their energies, then high again. Many Aquarians are extremely highly sexed and very clever and active in bed.

PISCES
20th February to 20th March

This idealistic, dreamy, kind and impractical sign needs a lot of understanding. They have a fractured personality which has so many sides and so many moods that they probably don't even understand themselves. Nobody is more kind, thoughtful and caring, but they have a tendency to drift away from people and responsibilities. When the going gets rough, they get going! Being creative, clever and resourceful, these people can achieve a great deal and really reach the top, but few of them do. Some Pisceans have a self-destruct button which they press before reaching their goal. Others do achieve success and the motivating force behind this essentially spiritual and mystical sign is often money. Many Pisceans feel insecure, most suffer some experience of poverty at some time in their early lives and they grow into adulthood determined that they will never feel that kind of uncertainty again.

Pisceans are at home in any kind of creative or caring career. Many can be found in teaching, nursing and the arts. Some find life hard and are often unhappy; many have to make tremendous sacrifices on behalf of others. This may be a pattern which repeats itself from childhood, where the message is that the Piscean's needs always come last. These people can be stubborn, awkward, selfish and quite nasty when a friendship or relationship goes sour. This is because, despite their basically kind and gentle personality, there is a side which needs to be in charge of any relationship. Pisceans make extremely faithful partners as long as the romance doesn't evaporate and their partners treat them well. Problems occur if they are mistreated or rejected, if they become bored or restless or if their alcohol intake climbs over the danger level. The Piscean lover is a sexual fantasist, so in this sphere of life anything can happen!

SCORPIO

You and Yours

What is it like to bring up an Arien child? What kind of father does a Libran make? How does it feel to grow up with a Sagittarian mother? Whatever your own sign is, how do you appear to your parents and how do you behave towards your children?

THE SCORPIO FATHER

These fathers can be really awful or absolutely wonderful, and there aren't any half-measures. Good Scorpio men provide love and security because they stick closely to their homes and families and are unlikely to do a disappearing act. Difficult ones can be loud and tyrannical. These proud men want their children to be the best.

THE SCORPIO MOTHER

These mothers are either wonderful or not really maternal at all, although they try to do their best. If they take to child-rearing, they encourage their offspring educationally and in their hobbies. These mothers have no time for whiny or miserable children but they respect outgoing, talented and courageous ones, and can cope with a handful.

THE SCORPIO CHILD

Scorpio children are competitive, self-centred and unwilling to co-operate with brothers, sisters, teachers or anyone else when in an awkward mood. They can be deeply unreadable, living in a world of their own and filled with all kinds of strange angry feelings. At other times, they can be delightfully caring companions. They love animals, sports, children's organizations and group activities.

THE ARIES FATHER

Arien men take the duties of fatherhood very seriously. They read to their children, take them on educational trips and expose them to art and music from an early age. They can push their children too hard or tyrannize the sensitive ones. The Aries father wants his children not only to have what he didn't have but also to be what he isn't. He respects those children who are high achievers and who can stand up to him.

THE ARIES MOTHER

Arien women love their children dearly and will make amazing sacrifices for them, but don't expect them to give up their jobs or their outside interests for motherhood. Competitive herself, this mother wants her children to be the best and she may push them too hard. However, she is kind-hearted, affectionate and not likely to over-discipline them. She treats her offspring as adults and is well loved in return.

THE ARIES CHILD

Arien children are hard to ignore. Lively, noisy and demanding, they try to enjoy every moment of their childhood. Despite this, they lack confidence and need reassurance. Often clever but lacking in self-discipline, they need to be made to attend school each day and to do their homework. Active and competitive, these children excel in sports, dancing or learning to play a pop music instrument.

THE TAURUS FATHER

This man cares deeply for his children and wants the best for them, but doesn't expect the impossible. He may lay the law down and he can be unsympathetic to the attitudes and interests of a new generation. He may frighten young children by shouting at them. Being a responsible parent, he offers a secure family base but he may find it hard to let them go when they want to leave.

THE TAURUS MOTHER

These women make good mothers due to their highly domesticated nature. Some are real earth mothers, baking bread and making wonderful toys and games for their children. Sane and sensible but not highly imaginative, they do best with a child who has ordinary needs and they get confused by those who are 'special' in any way. Taurus mothers are very loving but they use reasonable discipline when necessary.

THE TAURUS CHILD

Taurean children can be surprisingly demanding. Their loud voices and stubborn natures can be irritating. Plump, sturdy and strong, some are shy and retiring, while others can bully weaker children. Artistic, sensual and often musical, these children can lose themselves in creative or beautiful hobbies. They need to be encouraged to share and express love and also to avoid too many sweet foods.

THE GEMINI FATHER

Gemini fathers are fairly laid back in their approach and, while they cope well with fatherhood, they can become bored with home life and try to escape from their duties. Some are so absorbed with work that they hardly see their offspring. At home, Gemini fathers will provide books, educational toys and as much computer equipment as the child can use, and they enjoy a family game of tennis.

THE GEMINI MOTHER

These mothers can be very pushy because they see education as the road to success. They encourage a child to pursue any interest and will sacrifice time and money for this. They usually have a job outside the home and may rely on other people to do some child-minding for them. Their children cannot always count on coming home to a balanced meal, but they can talk to their mothers on any subject.

THE GEMINI CHILD

These children needs a lot of reassurance because they often feel like square pegs in round holes. They either do very well at school and incur the wrath of less able children, or they fail dismally and have to make it up later in life. They learn to read early and some have excellent mechanical ability while others excel at sports. They get bored very easily and they can be extremely irritating.

THE CANCER FATHER

A true family man who will happily embrace even stepchildren as if they were his own. Letting go of the family when they grow up is another matter. Cancerian sulks, moodiness and bouts of childishness can confuse or frighten some children, while his changeable attitude to money can make them unsure of what they should ask for. This father enjoys domesticity and child-rearing and he may be happy to swap roles.

THE CANCER MOTHER

Cancerian women are excellent home makers and cheerful and reasonable mothers, as long as they have a part-time job or an interest outside the house. They instinctively know when a child is unhappy and can deal with it in a manner which is both efficient and loving. These women have a reputation for clinging but most are quite realistic when the time comes for their brood to leave the nest.

THE CANCER CHILD

These children are shy, cautious and slow to grow up. They may achieve little at school, 'disappearing' behind louder and more demanding classmates. They can be worriers who complain about every ache and pain or suffer from imaginary fears. They may take on the mother's role in the family, dictating to their sisters and brothers at times. Gentle and loving but moody and secretive, they need a lot of love and encouragement.

THE LEO FATHER

These men can be wonderful fathers as long as they remember that children are not simply small and rather obstreperous adults. Leo fathers like to be involved with their children and encourage them to do well at school. They happily make sacrifices for their children and they truly want them to have the best, but they can be a bit too strict and they may demand too high a standard.

THE LEO MOTHER

Leo mothers are very caring and responsible but they cannot be satisfied with a life of pure domesticity, and need to combine motherhood with a job. These mothers don't fuss about minor details. They're prepared to put up with a certain amount of noise and disruption, but they can be irritable and they may demand too much of their children.

THE LEO CHILD

These children know almost from the day they are born that they are special. They are usually loved and wanted but they are also aware that a lot is expected from them. Leo children appear outgoing but they are surprisingly sensitive and easily hurt. They only seem to wake up to the need to study a day or so after they leave school, but they find a way to make a success of their lives.

THE VIRGO FATHER

These men may be embarrassed by open declarations of love and affection and find it hard to give cuddles and reassurance to small children. Yet they love their offspring dearly and will go to any lengths to see that they have the best possible education and outside activities. Virgoan men can become wrapped up in their work, forgetting to spend time relaxing and playing with their children.

THE VIRGO MOTHER

Virgoan women try hard to be good mothers because they probably had a poor childhood themselves. They love their children very much and want the best for them but they may be fussy about unnecessary details, such as dirt on the kitchen floor or the state of the children's school books. If they can keep their tensions and longings away from their children, they can be the most kindly and loving parents.

THE VIRGO CHILD

Virgoan children are practical and capable and can do very well at school, but they are not always happy. They don't always fit in and they may have difficulty making friends. They may be shy, modest and sensitive and they can find it hard to live up to their own impossibly high standards. Virgo children don't need harsh discipline, they want approval and will usually respond perfectly well to reasoned argument.

THE LIBRA FATHER

Libran men mean well, but they may not actually perform that well. They have no great desire to be fathers but welcome their children when they come along. They may slide out of the more irksome tasks by having an absorbing job or a series of equally absorbing hobbies which keep them occupied outside the home. These men do better with older children because they can talk to them.

THE LIBRA MOTHER

Libran mothers are pleasant and easy-going but some of them are more interested in their looks, their furnishings and their friends than their children. Others are very loving and kind but a bit too soft, which results in their children disrespecting them or walking all over them in later life. These mothers enjoy talking to their children and encouraging them to succeed.

THE LIBRA CHILD

These children are charming and attractive and they have no difficulty in getting on with people. They make just enough effort to get through school and only do the household jobs they cannot dodge. They may drive their parents mad with their demands for the latest gadget or gimmick. However, their common sense, sense of humour and reasonable attitude makes harsh discipline unnecessary.

THE SAGITTARIUS FATHER

Sagittarian fathers will give their children all the education they can stand. They happily provide books, equipment and take their offspring out to see anything interesting. They may not always be available to their offspring, but they make up for it by surprising their families with tickets for sporting events or by bringing home a pet for the children. These men are cheerful and childlike themselves.

THE SAGITTARIUS MOTHER

This mother is kind, easy-going and pleasant. She may be very ordinary with suburban standards or she may be unbelievably eccentric, forcing the family to take up strange diets and filling the house with weird and wonderful people. Some opt out of child-rearing by finding childminders while others take on other people's children and a host of animals in addition to their own.

THE SAGITTARIUS CHILD

Sagittarian children love animals and the outdoor life but they are just as interested in sitting around and watching the telly as the next child. These children have plenty of friends whom they rush out and visit at every opportunity. Happy and optimistic but highly independent, they cannot be pushed in any direction. Many leave home in late their teens in order to travel.

THE CAPRICORN FATHER

These are true family men who cope with housework and child-rearing but they are sometimes too involved in work to spend much time at home. Dutiful and caring, these men are unlikely to run off with a bimbo or to leave their family wanting. However, they can be stuffy or out of touch with the younger generation. They encourage their children to do well and to behave properly.

THE CAPRICORN MOTHER

Capricorn women make good mothers but they may be inclined to fuss. Being ambitious, they want their children to do well and they teach them to respect teachers, youth leaders and so on. These mothers usually find work outside the home in order to supplement the family income. They are very loving but they can be too keen on discipline and the careful management of pocket money.

THE CAPRICORN CHILD

Capricorn children are little adults from the day they are born. They don't need much discipline or encouragement to do well at school. Modest and well behaved, they are almost too good to be true. However, they suffer badly with their nerves and can be prone to ailments such as asthma. They need to be taught to let go, have fun and enjoy their childhood. Some are too selfish or ambitious to make friends.

THE AQUARIAN FATHER

Some Aquarian men have no great desire to be fathers but they make a reasonable job of it when they have to. They cope best when their children are reasonable and intelligent but, if they are not, they tune out and ignore them. Some Aquarians will spend hours inventing games and toys for their children while all of them value education and try to push their children.

THE AQUARIAN MOTHER

Some of these mothers are too busy putting the world to rights to see what is going on in their own family. However, they are kind, reasonable and keen on education. They may be busy outside the house but they often take their children along with them. They are not fussy homemakers, and are happy to have all the neighbourhood kids in the house. They respect a child's dignity.

THE AQUARIAN CHILD

These children may be demanding when very young but they become much more reasonable when at school. They are easily bored and need outside interests. They have many friends and may spend more time in other people's homes than in their own. Very stubborn and determined, they make it quite clear from an early age that they intend to do things their own way. These children suffer from nerves.

THE PISCES FATHER

Piscean men fall into one of two categories. Some are kind and gentle, happy to take their children on outings and to introduce them to art, culture, music or sport. Others are disorganized and unpredictable. The kindly fathers don't always push their children. They encourage their kids to have friends and a pet or two.

THE PISCES MOTHER

Piscean mothers may be lax and absent-minded but they love their children and are usually loved in return. Many are too disorganized to run a perfect household so meals, laundry, etc. can be hit and miss, but their children prosper despite this, although many learn to reverse the mother/child roles. These mothers teach their offspring to appreciate animals and the environment.

THE PISCES CHILD

These sensitive children may find life difficult and they can get lost among stronger, more demanding brothers and sisters. They may drive their parents batty with their dreamy attitude and they can make a fuss over nothing. They need a secure and loving home with parents who shield them from harsh reality while encouraging them to develop their imaginative and psychic abilities.

SCORPIO

Your Rising Sign

WHAT IS A RISING SIGN?
Your rising sign is the sign of the zodiac which was climbing up over the eastern horizon the moment you were born. This is not the same as your Sun sign; your Sun sign depends upon your date of birth, but your rising sign depends upon the time of day that you were born, combined with your date and place of birth.

The rising sign modifies your Sun sign character quite considerably, so when you have worked out which is your rising sign, read pages 39–40 to see how it modifies your Sun sign. Then take a deeper look by going back to 'All the Other Sun Signs' on page 21 and read the relevant Sun sign material there to discover more about your ascendant (rising sign) nature.

One final point is that the sign that is opposite your rising sign (or 'ascendant') is known as your 'descendant'. This shows what you want from other people, and it may give a clue as to your choice of friends, colleagues and lovers (see pages 41–3). So once you have found your rising sign and read the character interpretation, check out the character reading for your descendant to see what you are looking for in others.

How to Begin
Read through this section while following the example below. Even if you only have a vague idea of your birth time, you won't find this method difficult; just go for a rough time of birth and then read the Sun sign information for that sign to see if it fits your personality. If you seem to be more like the sign that comes before or after it, then it is likely that you were born a little earlier or later than your assumed time of birth. Don't forget to deduct an hour for summertime births.

1. Look at the illustration top right. You will notice that it has the time of day arranged around the outer circle. It looks a bit like a clock face, but it is different because it shows the whole 24-hour day in two-hour blocks.

2. Write the astrological symbol that represents the Sun (a circle with a dot in the middle) in the segment that corresponds to your time of birth. (If you were born during Daylight Saving or British Summer Time, deduct one hour from your birth time.) Our example shows someone who was born between 2 a.m. and 4 a.m.

SCORPIO

3. Now write the name of your sign or the symbol for your sign on the line which is at the end of the block of time that your Sun falls into. Our example shows a person who was born between 2 a.m. and 4 a.m. under the sign of Pisces.

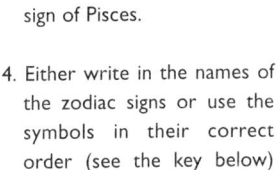

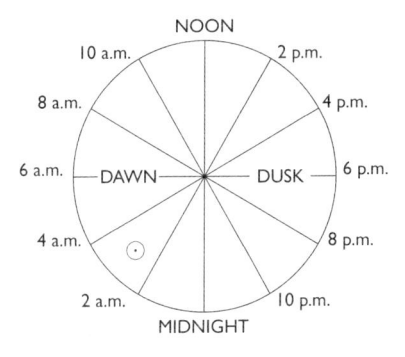

4. Either write in the names of the zodiac signs or use the symbols in their correct order (see the key below) around the chart in an anti-clockwise direction, starting from the line which is at the start of the block of time that your sun falls into.

5. The sign that appears on the left-hand side of the wheel at the 'Dawn' line is your rising sign, or ascendant. The example shows a person born with the Sun in Pisces and with Aquarius rising. Incidentally, the example chart also shows Leo, which falls on the 'Dusk' line, in the descendant. You will always find the ascendant sign on the 'Dawn' line and the descendant sign on the 'Dusk' line.

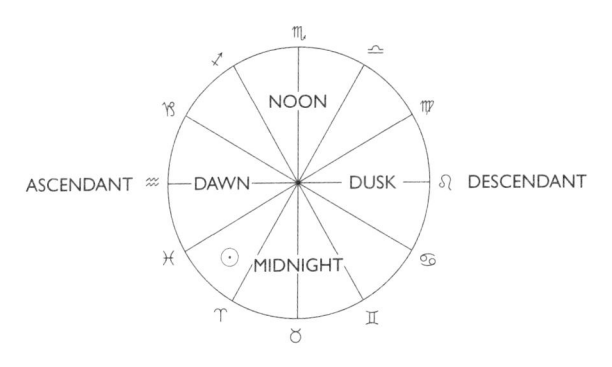

♈ Aries	♋ Cancer	♎ Libra	♑ Capricorn
♉ Taurus	♌ Leo	♏ Scorpio	♒ Aquarius
♊ Gemini	♍ Virgo	♐ Sagittarius	♓ Pisces

SCORPIO

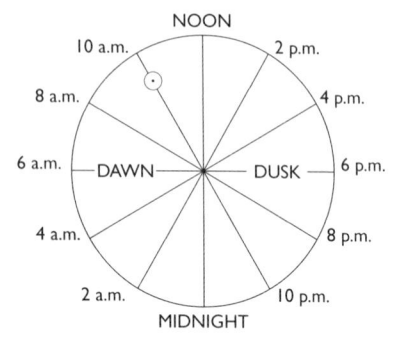

Here is another example for you to run through, just to make sure that you have grasped the idea correctly. This example is for a more awkward time of birth, being exactly on the line between two different blocks of time. This example is for a person with a Capricorn Sun sign who was born at 10 a.m.

1. The Sun is placed exactly on the 10 a.m. line.

2. The sign of Capricorn is placed on the 10 a.m. line.

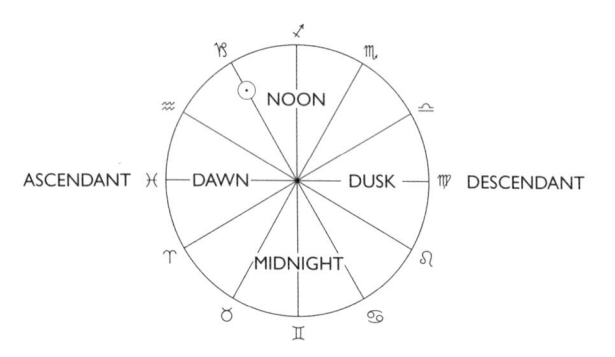

3. All the other signs are placed in astrological order (anti-clockwise) around the chart.

4. This person has the Sun in Capricorn and Pisces rising, and therefore with Virgo on the descendant.

SCORPIO

Using the Rising Sign Finder
Please bear in mind that this method is approximate. If you want to be really sure of your rising sign, you should contact an astrologer. However, this system will work with reasonable accuracy wherever you were born. Check out the Sun and ascendant combination in the following pages. Once you've done so, if you're not quite sure you've got it right, you should also read the Sun sign character readings on pages 21–8 for the signs both before and after the rising sign you think is yours. Rising signs are such an obvious part of one's personality that one quick glance will show you which one belongs to you.

Can Your Rising Sign Tell You More about Your Future?
When it comes to tracking events, the rising sign is equal in importance to the Sun sign. So, if you want a more accurate forecast when reading newspapers or magazines, you should read the horoscope for your rising sign as well as your Sun sign. In the case of books such as this, you should really treat yourself to two: one to correspond with your rising sign, and another for your usual Sun sign, and read both each day!

How Your Rising Sign Modifies Your Sun Sign

SCORPIO WITH ARIES RISING This powerful combination belongs to a soldier or a person who fights for truth and justice. However, this means that you may miss out a little on family life.

SCORPIO WITH TAURUS RISING You need to love and be loved, but you may have to wait until the right person comes along. You are stubborn but probably not hard to live with.

SCORPIO WITH GEMINI RISING You are attracted to work in an unusual field, such as forensics or some other kind of investigative job. Your nerves are delicate.

SCORPIO WITH CANCER RISING Home and family are important to

SCORPIO

you but you are also restless and love to travel over water. You have a great deal of charm and a likeable personality.

SCORPIO WITH LEO RISING This powerful combination makes you a true leader. You may choose a military life or something similar. You also have impossibly high standards.

SCORPIO WITH VIRGO RISING You are deeply intellectual and you may be keen on medical work or the creation of music or literature. You must watch your sharp tongue.

SCORPIO WITH LIBRA RISING This combination attracts you to legal work or at least to the idea of fair play for all. You could be interested in politics or in helping humanity.

SCORPIO WITH SCORPIO RISING This is Scorpio in its purest form. Your feelings are intensely passionate and you take life seriously. People either love you or hate you. You are even more intuitive if born after dawn, and rather more tough and outgoing if born before.

SCORPIO WITH SAGITTARIUS RISING You are drawn to mystical or psychic matters and you could be quite eccentric at times. You will travel and meet many interesting people.

SCORPIO WITH CAPRICORN RISING You need personal and financial security and you will work hard to get it. You are career-minded, but you also have a good social life.

SCORPIO WITH AQUARIUS RISING Work is important to you, and you could be drawn to medical or investigative work. You have plenty of friends and an interesting life. You may be stubborn at times.

SCORPIO WITH PISCES RISING Your feelings are very strong and also very sensitive. You fear loss or abandonment although you can enjoy your own company when you choose to.

SCORPIO

Scorpio in Love

YOU NEED:

LOYALTY You fear abandonment and you hate disloyalty in any form. If someone betrays your trust, you never believe in that person again.

RESPECT You need a partner whom you can respect and who respects you. You cannot take ridicule and you don't enjoy being in a relationship with a partner who tries to undermine you or who talks down to you in front of others.

PARTNERSHIP You can be the strong one in a relationship but you don't appreciate a lazy partner who leaves everything to you. You need to feel that you are being met half-way, and that he or she sees the importance of what you are trying to achieve.

YOU GIVE:

TRUTH You don't lie and you don't bend the truth. If you are not sure of your facts, you may say nothing at all, and you do have a tendency to keep your worries to yourself but, when asked, you will tell it as it is.

STEADFASTNESS You stick to a partner through thick and thin and you are a hundred per cent behind his or her endeavours. You work hard and you take relationships seriously.

PASSION You feel deeply about many things and you want a partner who is as committed as you are. Your sexual feelings are strong and you never leave a partner in doubt about your desire for him or her.

WHAT YOU CAN EXPECT FROM THE OTHER ZODIAC SIGNS:

ARIES *Truth, honesty, playfulness.* You can expect an open and honest relationship with no hidden agendas. Your Arien lover will be a bit childish at times, however.

TAURUS *Security, stability, comfort.* Taureans will stand by you and try to improve your financial position. They will create beautiful homes and gardens for their partners.

GEMINI *Stimulation, encouragement, variety.* Gemini lovers are never boring; they give encouragement and are always ready for an outing. They give emotional support too.

CANCER *Emotional security, companionship. help.* Cancerians will never leave you stranded at a party or alone when suffering from the flu. They always lend a hand when asked.

SCORPIO

- **LEO** *Affection, fun, loyalty.* Leo lovers are very steadfast and they would avenge anyone who hurt one of their family. They enjoy romping and playing affectionate love games.
- **VIRGO** *Clear-thinking, kindness, humour.* Virgoans make intelligent and amusing partners. They can be critical but are never unkind. They take their responsibility towards you seriously.
- **LIBRA** *Fair-play, sensuality, advice.* Librans will listen to your problems and give balanced and sensible advice. They are wonderfully inventive, and are affectionate lovers too.
- **SAGITTARIUS** *Honesty, fun, novelty.* These lovers will never bore you and they'll keep up with whatever pace you set. They seek the truth and they don't keep their feelings hidden.
- **CAPRICORN** *Companionship, common sense, laughter.* Capricorns enjoy doing things together and they won't leave you in the lurch when the going gets tough. They can make you laugh too.
- **AQUARIUS** *Stimulation, friendship, sexuality.* Aquarians are friends as well as lovers. They are great fun because you never know what they are going to do next, in or out of bed.
- **PISCES** *Sympathy, support, love.* These romantic lovers never let you down. They can take you with them into their personal fantasy world and they are always ready for a laugh.

WHICH SIGN ARE YOU COMPATIBLE WITH?

SCORPIO/ARIES
Hot sexual union but many arguments as each tries to dominate.

SCORPIO/TAURUS
Shared interests and outlook make this a good combination.

SCORPIO/GEMINI
Scorpio might be too dominant.

SCORPIO/CANCER
Much in common and a similar emotional outlook.

SCORPIO/LEO
This works well, both are playful and both love a bit of drama.

SCORPIO/VIRGO
This seems to be a disaster area with both being too critical.

SCORPIO/LIBRA
Not much in common for a love match but all right for work.

SCORPIO/SCORPIO
Either tremendous harmony or a fight to the death!

SCORPIO

SCORPIO/SAGITTARIUS
Sagittarius may be too unsettled for Scorpio.

SCORPIO/CAPRICORN
Capricorn can stand up to Scorpio so it works well.

SCORPIO/AQUARIUS
Both extremely obstinate and tense, could be a battleground.

SCORPIO/PISCES
Both emotional and intuitive, can have shared interests too.

Your Prospects for 1999

LOVE

Where your own feelings are concerned and also your personal relationship situation, this is likely to be an exciting if rather unsettled year. You seem to have gone through a rather static patch where love relationships are concerned which means that you have either been happy and settled in your partnership or alone with very little going on. Either way, things are likely to hot up for you this year. If you are settled, nothing is likely to change but your life within the partnership will be busy and full. You and your lover could start a business or some other kind of enterprise together. While this seems to get off to a very good start, things will then be delayed and held back until later in the year or even early next year. However, you will have to put a lot of work into the early preparatory stages of this. If you are alone, there will be opportunities to meet new people and to fall in love. The problem is that the other perso'is life looks complicated and he or she may not be free to make a full commitment to you at this time. Your own feelings of passion and excitement may blind you to the implications of what you are taking on and you could end up with a lover but also with all the baggage of his or her past life that has yet to be sorted out.

MONEY AND WORK

Both your working situation and your financial one look confusing this year. To take money first, it looks as though you will be the major earner and that your partner may not be able to contribute as much as you both would like once the year gets going. Happily, he or she won't land you with debts either, so it may all balance out in the end. You should be in a fairly good position financially, earning money from teaching or helping others in some way or another. Your job situation will go through massive ups and downs with great success on the way after a long period of struggle. You will be well thought of and you will have more responsibility piled upon you than is normally the case. An older person or someone in a position of authority will do a great deal to help you and he or she will have a good opinion of you. Money and opportunities will come through work-related matters. You may have to sign contracts or deal with other legal matters in connection with work and, if so, this should be all right. A job that seems to go on to the back burner from June to October comes back again in late October. However, there's a distinct possibility that you won't really see a successful result from all this until the very end of the year.

HEALTH

With Mars in your sign off and on this year, you should be full of energy and vigour but you will have to take care not to do things in a rash or hasty manner because Mars can bring accidents. Fevers and headaches are also possible, especially when Mars is in retrograde motion from late March to early June. The area of your chart that is devoted to health is actually very well starred and about the only real problem that may arise is that you could gain unwanted extra weight. However, sports, dancing or other active hobbies look as though they will be high on your agenda this year, so you may be able to nip the weight problem in the bud before it starts. It may be as well to get your eyes tested a little more frequently than usual now as Mars can affect one's sight.

FAMILY AND HOME

This is going to be a very unsettled area of your life this year mainly due to a series of eclipses that occur on the 31st of January, the 16th of February, the 28th of July and the 11th of August. Even without these events, your domestic circumstances look particularly unpredictable. You could suddenly decide to move house and this decision would be based on circumstances rather than by choice. Family members may suddenly leave your orbit while others could just as suddenly enter it. August looks like being a particularly difficult month with just about anything happening and probably with a series of events all occurring at the same time.

LUCK

Your working life will be lucky and successful for you this year and you could be given a good raise and plenty of recognition for what you do. Luck in connection with love could come your way for a short time during July but it could appear to slip away again after that for a few weeks. If you fancy making a wager or two, do this before mid-February as the early part of the year looks good for gambles and speculative ventures.

The Aspects and their Astrological Meanings

CONJUNCT	This shows important events which are usually, but not always, good.
SEXTILE	Good, particularly for work and mental activity.
SQUARE	Difficult, challenging.
TRINE	Great for romance, family life and creativity.
OPPOSITE	Awkward, depressing, challenging.
INTO	This shows when a particular planet enters a new sign of the zodiac, thus setting off a new phase or a new set of circumstances.
DIRECT	When a planet resumes normal direct motion.
RETROGRADE	When a planet apparently begins to go backwards.
VOID	When the Moon makes no aspect to any planet.

SCORPIO

September at a Glance

LOVE	♥	♥	♥
WORK	★	★	★
MONEY	£	£	£
HEALTH	☩		
LUCK	♘	♘	♘

TUESDAY, 1ST SEPTEMBER
Moon trine Saturn

There aren't many problems that can't be solved if you take the time to sit down and discuss them sensibly with your other half. A problem shared is a problem halved.

WEDNESDAY, 2ND SEPTEMBER
Void Moon

The term 'void of course' means that neither the Moon nor any of the other planets is making any important aspects during the course of its travels today. When this kind of day occurs, the worst thing you can do is to begin a new project. Do nothing special today except for routine tasks.

THURSDAY, 3RD SEPTEMBER
Moon conjunct Neptune

This will be gentle day on which you should give yourself over to the finer things of life. Read a good book and develop your knowledge or aesthetic tastes. Make the most of this Neptunian influence by listening to music or visiting an art gallery or museum.

FRIDAY, 4TH SEPTEMBER
Mars opposite Uranus

You may have the strongest desire to achieve a long-held ambition today, but if you are truly realistic in your assessment you'll know that this is not the right time to attempt it. Be particularly careful around machinery of any kind and be aware of health and safety regulations at all times.

SCORPIO

SATURDAY, 5TH SEPTEMBER
Moon opposite Venus

There's a see-saw of priorities today as the Moon opposes Venus bringing a crisis of conscience. We're not denying that there's plenty you should be doing in your professional life, yet there are family commitments that also need to be fulfilled. Your heart lies with the more personal side of your life but there are some duties that simply can't be shirked. Try to make the best of this, because you can't really win on both counts at once.

SUNDAY, 6TH SEPTEMBER
Full Moon eclipse

Today's Lunar eclipse could bring a bit of trouble your way. Eclipses only become significant when they coincide with a sensitive spot on one's own birthchart, so let's hope that today's eclipse passes you by without you even noticing!

MONDAY, 7TH SEPTEMBER
Moon sextile Neptune

If ever there was a day for a cuddle on the sofa, then this is it. You're sentimental, sensitive and extremely sensuous, so time spent with a lover should be fun. However, if there isn't a lover, a romantic novel or film will have to do!

TUESDAY, 8TH SEPTEMBER
Mercury into Virgo

The charitable impulses that make you such an endearing soul become a liability at the moment. Mercury moves into your eleventh Solar house now, making you the target for every plausible rogue with a story of woe. You are more than prepared to help, but make sure that any cause you support is genuine. At least you are assured of a convivial atmosphere with friends over the next few weeks.

WEDNESDAY, 9TH SEPTEMBER
Mercury trine Saturn

Bright, beautiful and clever, that's what you are today! Your mind is crystal clear and you are about to come up with the most amazing ideas. Your friends, your lover and everybody else around you will be amazed by your perspicacity.

THURSDAY, 10TH SEPTEMBER
Venus trine Saturn

Your emotions run high today. Venus and Saturn combine to suddenly overturn previously strong inhibitions and encourage you to passionately express your deeper feelings. A sudden infatuation could sweep you off your feet!

SCORPIO

FRIDAY, 11TH SEPTEMBER
Mercury conjunct Venus

Influential friends are a help to anyone but today such people will come rushing to your aid. You may be offered an unusual job or given an excellent opportunity to expand your experience of life.

SATURDAY, 12TH SEPTEMBER
Moon sextile Mars

The Moon makes a good aspect to Mars, so for those who are working today the career picture looks promising. This is not a time to ignore material affairs such as pension plans, insurance policies and other kinds of shared resources. A little attention paid to your long-term security should bring ample dividends.

SUNDAY, 13TH SEPTEMBER
Moon square Jupiter

Your passions are strong today, but not altogether wise. You may be torn between two lovers or generally feel some emotional conflict. If you are creatively inclined, you may experience an artistic block.

MONDAY, 14TH SEPTEMBER
Moon sextile Venus

The Moon's pleasing contact with Venus reminds you that you have so many friends that some of them get left behind or fall by the wayside as you make your path through life. Perhaps it's time you made the effort to get in touch again. If this involves travel – even foreign travel – then you can be sure of an abundant welcome.

TUESDAY, 15TH SEPTEMBER
Moon sextile Sun

You'll feel the urge to forget tradition and strike out on a new and independent course today. Travel seems very appealing now, especially if you've been under stress from your in-laws!

WEDNESDAY, 16TH SEPTEMBER
Sun opposite Jupiter

It doesn't matter how enthusiastic some of your friends are, you shouldn't be taken in by high-flown promises that are no more than hot air. It seems that some people have false expectations that will obviously come to grief. Words of caution won't dissuade them from their ill-advised course, but you don't have to follow them down the road to ruin, do you? Don't follow the crowd against your better judgement.

SCORPIO

THURSDAY, 17TH SEPTEMBER
Moon conjunct Mars

Steady how you go, because the Lunar aspect to Mars makes you too prone to impatience and irritability. You don't suffer fools gladly at the best of times, but when work colleagues seem wilfully stupid it's too much to bear. You may have to face a clash of egos now, but it's best to back down because false pride won't get you anywhere.

FRIDAY, 18TH SEPTEMBER
Moon trine Saturn

You know where you are going and what you want from life and fortunately your partners, associates and even your lover are completely in tune with your needs at this time.

SATURDAY, 19TH SEPTEMBER
Mercury opposite Jupiter

Don't be too willing to fall for the exaggerated claims of an excitable child or a friend who should really know better. Mercury, ruler of communication, is in opposition to Jupiter, which makes tall stories the norm rather than the exception. It's important that you keep your feet on the ground. Don't let others' fantasies tempt you into abandoning common sense.

SUNDAY, 20TH SEPTEMBER
New Moon

It's time to show the world what you're made of! The New Moon gives you a chance to show that you have the initiative and drive to push a project through to a successful conclusion. Anything that requires personal flair combined with the co-operation of colleagues will go well. Don't be afraid to make your mark; you can do anything you set your mind to, so believe in yourself.

MONDAY, 21ST SEPTEMBER
Moon sextile Pluto

You may think up some strange or off-beat way to make money now and this could very well work. You could be feeling sensitive now, so try to avoid the kind of situation that is guaranteed to upset you. You may be happier to spend the day among animals rather than people.

TUESDAY, 22ND SEPTEMBER
Sun trine Neptune

A short holiday could bring you far more than you had anticipated, and you may

SCORPIO

find yourself being swept off your feet by a bright and humorous lover! You will soon be faced with a major decision about your special relationship, and this could herald the end of a casual affair but the start of something deeper and more important. Your hopes and dreams should soon be realized.

WEDNESDAY, 23RD SEPTEMBER
Sun into Libra

The movement of the Sun into your Solar twelfth house suggests that the next month will be rather quiet and solitary. You may be quite busy on a day-to-day basis but behind this lies a need to retreat into yourself and reflect upon your progress. This is a wonderful time to repay anything that you owe to others, in the form of money, goods or other obligations.

THURSDAY, 24TH SEPTEMBER
Mercury into Libra

Mercury enters the quietest area of your Solar horoscope today, so do not expect much to happen in the way of business over the next few weeks. You may not feel much like talking and you may want to be alone more than usual. You may stay indoors because you are feeling off-colour, or because you simply need time to yourself.

FRIDAY, 25TH SEPTEMBER
Sun conjunct Mercury

You seem to be on a peculiarly spiritual journey just now. Perhaps you are actively studying something such as astrology, or reading something that is making you think of realms beyond or outside your normal experience of life.

SATURDAY, 26TH SEPTEMBER
Moon conjunct Pluto

There is a definite turning point now concerning your finances. You have probably had enough arguments over who owns what to last you a lifetime, and now is the time to get this settled for good. There may be a delay or a problem in connection with a contract or an agreement, but this matter should soon speed up.

SUNDAY, 27TH SEPTEMBER
Mercury sextile Pluto

If you feel the need to maintain a low profile, we think that you are right to do so. It also seems fortuitous to keep any details of your current financial position to yourself.

SCORPIO

MONDAY, 28TH SEPTEMBER
Moon trine Saturn

This is a wonderful day for presenting your ideas to others. If you want to speak about how you feel or make them understand what makes you tick, you will find just the right words to do so.

TUESDAY, 29TH SEPTEMBER
Sun sextile Pluto

You seem to be striking a nice balance between spiritual and practical values today. You may, for example, spend a little time examining your conscience and beliefs and then get on with some nice money-making projects.

WEDNESDAY, 30TH SEPTEMBER
Venus into Libra

Venus moves into your Solar twelfth house today, bringing a period of reflection and retreat. You may not want to do much socializing over the next month and you may seek your own company, or perhaps that of one trusted friend. Oddly enough, romantic matters and even out-and-out love affairs will prosper now, as long as you keep them quiet for the time being.

October at a Glance

LOVE	♥	♥	♥	
WORK	★	★	★	★
MONEY	£			
HEALTH	✛	✛	✛	✛
LUCK	♘	♘	♘	

THURSDAY, 1ST OCTOBER
Sun trine Uranus

A sudden and unexpected windfall could come your way today. However, this is more likely to come in the form of a bargain for the home – for example, you may find just the piece of furniture you are looking for advertised on the notice board in your local supermarket. You may find a bike for the kids, or perhaps a useful tool or gardening implement at just the right price.

SCORPIO

FRIDAY, 2ND OCTOBER
Moon opposite Mars

Don't be surprised if those around you are rather tense today. The Moon is opposed to Mars which shows that unruly emotions are about to come bubbling to the surface. You won't know the root cause of these irritable feelings, but the results are obvious enough. Steer clear of all domestic controversies today and you'll be less likely to respond to carping with a few hurtful home truths of your own.

SATURDAY, 3RD OCTOBER
Moon square Pluto

Cash-flow worries could give you sleepless nights if you weren't so preoccupied with other more pleasurable pursuits. However, money worries have to be addressed if you're to maintain your standard of living. Nothing is beyond you and all problems can be solved with a little diligence and attention to detail. So what are you waiting for?

SUNDAY, 4TH OCTOBER
Moon conjunct Jupiter

Love, luck and sunshine are on the way to you today. This would be a great day to take off for distant and exotic shores but if you can't do this, then get out and about as much as you can locally.

MONDAY, 5TH OCTOBER
Venus sextile Pluto

There's a terrible temptation to push the financial boat out too far today. Venus's self-indulgent angle to Pluto prompts you to spend more than you can afford on luxuries and pleasure. We know that you deserve a little treat now and again, but when the spending gets out of hand it's time to call a halt. Try to be sensible with the pennies.

TUESDAY, 6TH OCTOBER
Full Moon

Today's Full Moon is a heavenly signal to think carefully about your working life and day-to-day habits. If you aren't happy, then make up your mind to change things for the better. Of course, some opposition is to be expected from those who rather like the *status quo*, but you mustn't allow anyone else's opinions to sway you from a balanced judgement. If you are unemployed, you can be sure that your fortunes will change very soon.

SCORPIO

WEDNESDAY, 7TH OCTOBER
Mars into Virgo

Many of your most cherished dreams come a step closer to fulfilment as the red planet Mars enters your horoscopic area of hopes and wishes. You'll be endowed with the energy and drive to see your aims through to a successful conclusion. Male friends are especially important now, as they can point you in directions that you hadn't previously considered. This period should see a rapid upturn in your social life. Excitement follows where Mars leads!

THURSDAY, 8TH OCTOBER
Moon sextile Jupiter

It's important to think about activities and pleasures that you and a partner can share as this isn't a time for solitary occupations. You've got to show your other half what an important asset he or she is. You may wish to take up a hobby together or just make some time to enjoy more romantic and intimate times.

FRIDAY, 9TH OCTOBER
Moon trine Uranus

You may come up with a sensible way of increasing the value of your home today, and this may set you off on a course of building or decorating. The same goes for any other land or property that you own. Any property-related ideas could come from an acquaintance or an unusual outside source. Discuss these with your partner to see whether he or she agrees with them.

SATURDAY, 10TH OCTOBER
Mars trine Saturn

You may love your partner to death but there are times when you prefer the company of a friend. Today, you can enjoy both because you may spend a pleasant hour or two gossiping with your pals and then end the day in affectionate harmony with your lover.

SUNDAY, 11TH OCTOBER
Neptune direct

The planet Neptune returns to direct motion today bringing an extremely subtle, yet powerful influence to bear. Slowly, you'll find that perplexing problems will now seem straightforward. Even the most complex issues can be resolved because you'll be using your intuition. Neptune's forward motion should also help you to sort out your priorities.

SCORPIO

MONDAY, 12TH OCTOBER
Mercury into Scorpio

Mercury moves into your own sign for a while today, and this brings the start of a much more positive phase for you. You need to get down to brass tacks and deal with any outstanding business matters. Over the next three weeks or so you will spend a fair bit of time writing letters, phoning people and travelling around the neighbourhood in order to complete a number of small jobs.

TUESDAY, 13TH OCTOBER
Moon square Mercury

The pressures of life can be rather unbearable at times. Your thoughts are clouded by the Moon and Mercury now, so you need an ego boost to offset the criticism and lack of appreciation you've found recently in the workplace. We all need our dreams, so indulge yourself in something you really like – and never mind what anyone else thinks of it!

WEDNESDAY, 14TH OCTOBER
Mercury sextile Mars

This should be an exciting day when new things and people are about to enter your life and change it for the better. Mercury and Mars are in splendid aspect, urging you to seek out new friends. This is no time to be a wallflower, so go out and enjoy yourself. You'll find dazzling company and a lot of laughs.

THURSDAY, 15TH OCTOBER
Moon trine Saturn

An older relative or someone who is in a position of authority could be of considerable help to you today. You and your partner may have to work your way through a number of official or governmental regulations, and this older or wiser person could be just the one to help you.

FRIDAY, 16TH OCTOBER
Moon square Pluto

Your mood is at odds with the general atmosphere around you today. Everyone else may be happy and cheerful while you're feeling downhearted. Remember, there will be better days.

SATURDAY, 17TH OCTOBER
Mercury square Uranus

You could be a little too blunt for comfort today since you won't be able to see any earthly reason why you should keep your opinions to yourself!

SCORPIO

SUNDAY, 18TH OCTOBER
Uranus direct

The large and eccentric planet, Uranus, turns to direct motion today ending a period of unpredictable events in your family circle. There have been reasons for some of your loved ones' strange behaviour but, because you didn't know what these were, it has been hard to understand their activities. All will become clear over the next few weeks.

MONDAY, 19TH OCTOBER
Mars square Pluto

There are rumblings of discontent amongst your friends now as the harsh aspect between Mars and Pluto has repercussions on your social life. A quarrel is imminent, and if you're wise you'll keep well out of it or it'll cost you in terms of prestige and ego damage. If you actually are a protagonist in a dispute, then don't expect it to be solved easily or without sacrifice. One side's as bad as the other in this little conflict.

TUESDAY, 20TH OCTOBER
New Moon

A New Moon in the most psychic area of your chart suggests that the next month will bring you closer to intuitive, psychic and spiritual matters than ever before. You may have prophetic dreams or strange feelings that seem to portend future events. Areas of life that you have never explored before may suddenly become significant.

WEDNESDAY, 21ST OCTOBER
Moon square Uranus

Your mind is working overtime at the moment and you could have some really bright ideas. The problem is that others may not be as keen on your notions as you are, and if this is the case, you will have to guard against being too dogmatic in your approach. You may decide that you want to be accepted on an educational course, only to find that it is oversubscribed or wrong for you in some other way.

THURSDAY, 22ND OCTOBER
Sun square Neptune

You could find yourself in a rather vulnerable state today. The Sun's negative aspect to Neptune puts you at a disadvantage since your mind will not be firing on all cylinders. You need to take things slowly now, and try not to indulge in idle daydreams.

SCORPIO

FRIDAY, 23RD OCTOBER
Sun into Scorpio

The Sun is moving into your sign and this brings a number of goodies along with it. Birthday time means presents and parties and finding out who your friends are from the kind of birthday cards they send. Otherwise, a quiet day.

SATURDAY, 24TH OCTOBER
Venus into Scorpio

There's an upsurge in optimism today as Venus, planet of love, enters your own sign. This should put a much-needed sparkle back into your personality, and you'll find your popularity increases over the coming weeks. You can't fail to charm all around you, for who could resist your smouldering looks and magnetic attraction? Charisma is your middle name from now on, so make the most of it.

SUNDAY, 25TH OCTOBER
Saturn into Pisces retrograde

You could feel rather vulnerable today. The planet Saturn is to blame for this outbreak of doubt and anxiety so you'll need someone understanding to bolster your flagging self-confidence. Most of your worries seem to centre on money.

MONDAY, 26TH OCTOBER
Sun conjunct Venus

The embrace of the Sun and Venus shows that you are in a distinctly amorous frame of mind, and are in no mood for refusal of your advances. You might get the idea that we're saying that you're vain ... and you'd be right!

TUESDAY, 27TH OCTOBER
Moon sextile Mercury

Your mind turns to true spiritual values today. You may not be interested in organized religion but certain eternal truths seem so obvious to you now. If you discuss these matters, you'll find that others share your views if in original or unorthodox ways.

WEDNESDAY, 28TH OCTOBER
Moon square Sun

This is a strange day on which there could be good and bad news. However, the good news is likely to be really spectacular while the bad news, merely irritating. Your confidence may take a slight knock either because you say or do something silly or you are caught out looking less than your best.

SCORPIO

THURSDAY, 29TH OCTOBER
Saturn square Neptune

Your get-up-and-go looks as though it's got up and gone today as the gloomy planet Saturn gets a grip on your sex life! To put it mildly, things will not go too well. On the other hand, this is a temporary blip and will soon pass. Try not to be oversensitive about it.

FRIDAY, 30TH OCTOBER
Moon sextile Saturn

Although there's plenty that you could be getting on with and you know in your heart of hearts that you should be doing something productive, friends and neighbours are constantly making demands. Perhaps they want to use you as a sounding board for their ideas and plans, yet although you are prepared to listen your mind strays back to the mountain of tasks you've got to get through. A disrupted schedule is on the cards.

SATURDAY, 31ST OCTOBER
Moon conjunct Jupiter

What a fabulous day for indulging yourself and all your family in your favourite pastimes in the comfort of your own home. You don't have to venture out for an excellent time because you'll be more likely to find it in your own living room.

November at a Glance

LOVE	♥	♥	♥	♥	
WORK	★	★			
MONEY	£	£	£	£	£
HEALTH	☉	☉	☉		
LUCK	U	U	U	U	U

SUNDAY, 1ST NOVEMBER
Mercury into Sagittarius

Mercury's entry into your Solar house of possessions and finance turns your attention to economic realities. If you feel you've been overspending, then the next few weeks should help you sort out a practical financial strategy to put your

SCORPIO

savings back on an even keel. The keen insight that Mercury provides shows that this is a good opportunity to add to your cash resources.

MONDAY, 2ND NOVEMBER
Void Moon

There are no important planetary aspects today and even the Moon is unaspected. This kind of a day is called a 'void of course Moon' day, because the Moon is void of aspects during this part of its course. The best way to approach such a day is to do what is normal and natural for you without starting anything new or particularly special.

TUESDAY, 3RD NOVEMBER
Moon square Neptune

It's a worrying sort of day under the influence of the Moon and Neptune. Everything seems rather pessimistic as you consider your abilities and worry if you are up to the challenges that await you. Try to be more realistic because the picture isn't as grim as you believe. If you take an objective look at your life, you'll see that there's plenty to be hopeful about.

WEDNESDAY, 4TH NOVEMBER
Full Moon

Today's Full Moon highlights your personal relationships and urges you to discard anything that's getting in the way of a complete understanding with your partner. In strong relationships this is nothing to be afraid of, yet many will find that a whole chapter of your life is about to close. Full Moons show that the past is dead and gone, so don't cling to the old and accept the new in the certainty that the future will be better.

THURSDAY, 5TH NOVEMBER
Moon trine Neptune

You and a close friend or partner will be totally in tune with each other today. Communication becomes almost instinctive as you both experience an intimacy that is akin to telepathy.

FRIDAY, 6TH NOVEMBER
Mercury conjunct Pluto

You can't fail to profit by today's conjunction of Mercury and Pluto. This occurs in your area of finances, encouraging you to make the most of new and even revolutionary ways of making cash. You can plan the most cunning strategies now.

SCORPIO

SATURDAY, 7TH NOVEMBER
Mars opposite Jupiter

Wild passions could carry you away in total abandon today if you are particularly lucky. It may not be the best course of action by any means, yet you won't be complaining and will be prepared to face the music when the time comes.

SUNDAY, 8TH NOVEMBER
Venus trine Jupiter

It's a very fortunate day all around for you. The planets Venus and Jupiter are in wonderful aspect and this can only mean good luck, laughter and enjoyment. All emotional affairs will flourish now, because you're outgoing and excellent company. Your inhibitions have flown, so you can now show tremendous affection and receive it back a thousandfold. If you're going out socially, pick a different venue because you'll benefit from a change of scene.

MONDAY, 9TH NOVEMBER
Venus sextile Mars

This is a great day for being with other people. Friends, lovers and family will all be happy to share your company and cheer you up. You will bring them just as much pleasure in return.

TUESDAY, 10TH NOVEMBER
Sun trine Jupiter

This is be a wonderful day to indulge yourself and your family in something sporting. Take the kids to see a match or give encouragement by joining them in a game of volleyball.

WEDNESDAY, 11TH NOVEMBER
Moon square Venus

Work isn't exactly conducive to your frame of mind, but it won't do to let your duties slide completely. There are lots of things to do, and although you can't really be bothered with boring tasks you're going to have to knuckle down for today at least. Apparent goodwill from a boss or other authority figure may not live up to your expectations, so keep your nose to the grindstone.

THURSDAY, 12TH NOVEMBER
Moon square Pluto

You feel the need to keep some control over your finances now but your friends are encouraging you to go out and spend money like water. You may do a bit of both today.

SCORPIO

FRIDAY, 13TH NOVEMBER
Jupiter direct

The going should be much easier in affairs of the heart from now on. Today the influence of Jupiter ensures that this will the be the start of a level patch in all emotional affairs. In creative affairs too, your talents will shine and you'll find a ready appreciation of your personality and abilities. Expect some news concerning a pregnancy or a birth in the near future.

SATURDAY, 14TH NOVEMBER
Sun sextile Mars

If you are in a bit of a jam today, try asking one of your male friends to help you out. You may need to borrow some equipment or even a vehicle at rather short notice and it looks as if your pals will be able to assist you considerably.

SUNDAY, 15TH NOVEMBER
Moon sextile Mercury

Don't be in a rush to splash out on anything too expensive today. If you are patient, you will find a better deal. Think through financial matters carefully.

MONDAY, 16TH NOVEMBER
Moon opposite Saturn

You may not be feeling at your best today, so slow down, take some time off and mollycoddle yourself a little. You may have the start of a cold or another ailment, such as backache, could be plaguing you. This isn't likely to be a great day as far as work is concerned, so take some time off if you can.

TUESDAY, 17TH NOVEMBER
Venus into Sagittarius

The entry of Venus into Sagittarius will do your financial fortunes the world of good over the next couple of weeks. This is the start of a profitable time when money will come to you more easily than in the recent past. The true value of things too becomes an issue, and you'll realize that quality of life is equally as important as making cash. You'll desire tasteful surroundings and comfort while Venus remains in your house of possessions.

WEDNESDAY, 18TH NOVEMBER
Moon trine Jupiter

The Moon makes a marvellous aspect to lucky Jupiter today. You will be feeling on top of the world, looking good and oozing charm! All romantic affairs will do extremely well under this optimistic influence.

SCORPIO

THURSDAY, 19TH NOVEMBER
New Moon

Today's New Moon gives a considerable boost to your self-confidence and personal abilities. You may now feel that a change of image is overdue, so make a resolution to update your wardrobe, have a new hairdo and otherwise alter your appearance to match the exciting and outgoing person you know yourself to be.

FRIDAY, 20TH NOVEMBER
Mercury square Jupiter

There's only one thing worse than being wrong, and that's being right, especially when you're smug and superior. Be aware that an overly critical attitude will not earn you respect. Remember that pride comes before a fall so when tables turn, as they inevitably will, you'll be the one eating humble pie!

SATURDAY, 21ST NOVEMBER
Mercury retrograde

Although generally this is a good period for your financial prospects, short-term prospects take a downturn when Mercury goes into retrograde motion in one of the most sensitive economic areas of your chart. Keep a tight grip on your cash now, since impulsive spending will give you plenty of cause for regret later. A disappointing bank statement could reinforce you commitment to tighten the belt for a while.

SUNDAY, 22ND NOVEMBER
Sun into Sagittarius

The entry of the Sun into your financial sector is bound to be good news for your bank balance, and the next month will show a rapid increase in your wealth. To make the best of this Solar opportunity you'd better dust off the account books and take a good look at the figures. We're sure that there are expenses to cut and investments to make that will generally improve the situation. By the end of this exercise you should find that there is more cash to go around.

MONDAY, 23RD NOVEMBER
Venus conjunct Pluto

There should be quite a bit of extra money coming your way today. Rather than a windfall, this may be something that you have worked for and expect, but it's welcome all the same.

SCORPIO

TUESDAY, 24TH NOVEMBER
Moon sextile Sun

Home life and comfort move to centre stage today as the Moon makes a positive aspect to the Sun. All those luxuries that you crave may come a step nearer as you realize that you can afford to treat yourself. Perhaps some new furniture is in the offing.

WEDNESDAY, 25TH NOVEMBER
Venus sextile Uranus

Today should be busy and sociable as friends and relatives drop in for tea, coffee, chats and sympathy all day long. It may not be the peaceful day you had envisaged, but you'll still enjoy their company.

THURSDAY, 26TH NOVEMBER
Moon sextile Saturn

Whether your main interests lie at home or at work, today will be successful. While it is true that chores of one kind or another will occupy your mind and your time, there is a certain satisfaction to be derived from getting them over and done with. This will leave you free to put your energies elsewhere over the next few days.

FRIDAY, 27TH NOVEMBER
Neptune into Aquarius

The watery planet Neptune moves into your area of domesticity and tradition from today. The deep sensitivities of this planet will add to the harmony of your home and increase the happiness of your family.

SATURDAY, 28TH NOVEMBER
Mars trine Neptune

The positive aspect between Mars and Neptune will make you aware of an ideal or a worthy cause that you'd like to be involved in. You'll be moved by the plight of those less fortunate than yourself and will wish to do something concrete to help. You're convinced that a better world is possible and you'll be determined to contribute. Perhaps you could organize a fund-raising event to further your cause.

SUNDAY, 29TH NOVEMBER
Sun conjunct Pluto

You really should sit down and work out a sensible budget for the coming months. If you are in a relationship or a business partnership, then shared resources need to be discussed as well.

SCORPIO

MONDAY, 30TH NOVEMBER
Moon conjunct Saturn

There will be good news for you at work today. You may be given a raise, a promotion or a word or two of praise from a superior. You will look back on work that you have completed and you will be pleased with the results. This is a good time to finish one round of work and to start on another, so get going on new projects at work and in the home.

December at a Glance

LOVE	♥	♥	
WORK	★		
MONEY	£	£	£
HEALTH	✛	✛	
LUCK	♘	♘	♘

TUESDAY, 1ST DECEMBER
Mercury sextile Uranus

There's a change of mood on the home front today. A sense of growing excitement is evident as a major event is about to occur. You and your family will be caught up in a marvellous feeling of anticipation.

WEDNESDAY, 2ND DECEMBER
Sun sextile Uranus

You could experience some kind of breakthrough today. This may be a stroke of genius on your behalf or a really cracking idea that is put to you by a friend. The outcome could be an opportunity to increase your funds. If you are looking for a new place to live, you could stumble across the just the right property today and, what is more, this could happen in the most bizarre manner.

THURSDAY, 3RD DECEMBER
Full Moon

Today's Full Moon gives you a chance to shrug off some inhibitions that you learned early on, and haven't quite ditched. In sexual matters, you could learn a thing or two if you open your mind. Be prepared to respond to a loved one's

SCORPIO

overtures in a sympathetic manner – you'll probably enjoy the experience! Apart from your intimate life, the Full Moon provides the opportunity to put your financial affairs on a firm footing. Unspoken understandings won't wash any more, so make sure you are crystal clear in all you say.

FRIDAY, 4TH DECEMBER
Moon opposite Venus

Don't be taken in by attractive offers or apparent bargains today, because you'll find that for every cent saved you'll pay a dollar in repair bills. Shoddy goods and glib promises are the main dangers so don't allow yourself to be gullible or fall for attractive packaging. Curb any desire to spend beyond your means.

SATURDAY, 5TH DECEMBER
Mercury sextile Mars

You'll be full of enthusiasm today. Dreams you once thought were totally unrealistic will now be seen to be achievable. You'll look to the future with renewed confidence and the utter conviction that with a little luck and effort you can make your dreams come true!

SUNDAY, 6TH DECEMBER
Moon trine Jupiter

This is a very fortunate day as the Moon and Jupiter combine to shower you with opportunities. Dreary routine will be abandoned while you've got a taste for adventure. You may have a strong inclination to travel, yet you're unlikely to get any major plans off the ground just yet. At least there are plenty of new experiences in store.

MONDAY, 7TH DECEMBER
Moon sextile Mars

Ladies who happen to be reading this can expect a rather pleasant flirtation with a nice man at their place of work. Those of you who have social or career-based ambitions will have a very good day today, because your status among your colleagues and in your community is about to be enhanced.

TUESDAY, 8TH DECEMBER
Moon trine Sun

Monday's influence continues as your status is about to be raised to fresh heights. You may be on the point of promotion at work or of being well thought of in some other sphere of life. Even within the family, you could start to be seen as a person of substance and importance. Nice change for the better, isn't it?

SCORPIO

WEDNESDAY, 9TH DECEMBER
Venus trine Saturn

Some serious thought about your financial future would not go amiss today. Setting up a savings scheme into which you make regular contributions would be a very good idea.

THURSDAY, 10TH DECEMBER
Moon square Sun

Try to rein in needless expenditure now. Some friends may think you're a stick-in-the-mud, but you of all people know the value of money in the bank. It doesn't grow on trees, so don't act as if your bank is some sort of orchard!

FRIDAY, 11TH DECEMBER
Venus into Capricorn

The entry of Venus into your Solar house of communication adds charm and an ability to win your own way by persuasion alone. Someone will be very attracted by your opinions, so a more than passing interest will be awakened by a casual conversation. Short journeys too are going to be fortunate, leading too much-needed (and quite painless) life lessons.

SATURDAY, 12TH DECEMBER
Mars sextile Pluto

Strategy and financial planning are the favoured activities for today. You need to think about your financial realities and assess your incomings and outgoings. You'll probably find that there are better rates of interest to be had for loans, and various small debts that you can dispense with.

SUNDAY, 13TH DECEMBER
Moon sextile Sun

A final rethink before you splash out on something expensive will reveal that you have forgotten something. Don't worry though, you've still got time to make that final purchase. You could get a surprise gift, too.

MONDAY, 14TH DECEMBER
Moon sextile Venus

It would be a marvellous idea to get away from the rat race today. The Lunar aspect to Venus shows that your mind isn't on worldly duties so you may as well relax that fevered brow and try to renew your energies by taking it easy. It doesn't matter what you do to pass the time as long as you enjoy yourself. Perhaps you should indulge in a little luxury as the treat would do you good.

SCORPIO

TUESDAY, 15TH DECEMBER
Mars trine Uranus

There's no point charging in and trying to organize everyone else today. You need to be calm, think things through and work out the best moves just as if you were playing chess. Good opportunities are coming up, but how best to use them is your decision.

WEDNESDAY, 16TH DECEMBER
Moon sextile Neptune

Your opinions will win a lot of favour today. You will be charming and eloquent especially when talking about your own visions of the future and how things might be. An intellectual link may become physical!

THURSDAY, 17TH DECEMBER
Moon sextile Uranus

There should be a sudden and unexpected windfall for you or for some other family member. What seems certain is that if such a windfall does arrive, you will spend it on household goods or on relatives. Don't forget to treat yourself as well. You may feel like breaking out of a rut and having a bit of freedom now, but you are actually most likely to spend any free time in or near your home.

FRIDAY, 18TH DECEMBER
New Moon

The New Moon in your house of finance and possessions encourages you to re-evaluate everything that you regard as important. You may find that you've been basing your ideas of success on envy of others and judging your own accomplishments by those things that you own. Perhaps you've already achieved a level of security and are now looking for another challenge. Your future economic fortunes depend on your actions now, so maybe a bank manager or financial expert could help you get your ideas into perspective. Improvements are not only possible but likely over the next few weeks.

SATURDAY, 19TH DECEMBER
Sun trine Saturn

Financial and work problems ease today as the Sun breaks through the clouds of gloom. Problems will now be easier to solve and you will gain a renewed self-confidence.

SCORPIO

SUNDAY, 20TH DECEMBER
Moon square Mars

There could be some strange reason for the extra expense that you seem to be stuck with at the moment. Ill-health in your circle could be preventing you or some other member of your family from working, or you may lose work as a result of someone else's health problem. You may have to pay out for dental treatment, osteopathy or something similar at this time.

MONDAY, 21ST DECEMBER
Mercury conjunct Pluto

Don't allow others to talk you into doing something that you really feel is wrong for you. If you can avoid lending anything today, then do so. On the other hand, guard against manipulating others for your own ends now. If something needs to be changed, you'll have the courage to do it now.

TUESDAY, 22ND DECEMBER
Sun into Capricorn

This is the start of a rather busy period in which you will be dealing with correspondence, getting on the telephone and rushing around your neighbourhood at top speed. For the next month or so, your days will be filled with activity and you will be buzzing from one job to another like a demented bee. Enjoy the success and the achievement that this brings, but do remember to relax a little from time to time.

WEDNESDAY, 23RD DECEMBER
Mercury sextile Uranus

Good news connected with money is due today, and you could find that you will be very much better off, no matter how unlikely this prospect seems. A relative too may receive a windfall.

THURSDAY, 24TH DECEMBER
Moon square Pluto

Children may be costing you too much in terms of time, money or energy and you may have to be realistic about this – even if it is Christmas Eve! You may have to reconsider educational plans for your children or cut down what you spend on them in terms of gifts, treats or outings.

FRIDAY, 25TH DECEMBER
Moon conjunct Jupiter

If you're young at heart this is going to be an excellent Christmas Day! The Lunar

SCORPIO

conjunction with Jupiter in your area of fun, leisure activities and romance brings a ray of pure joy into your life. Of course having so much fun is bound to cost money, but you won't be worried about that. You'd rather leave boring thoughts of finance to another day.

SATURDAY, 26TH DECEMBER
Moon square Sun

You are going to spend a lot of time on the phone over the next month or so and you will also have a pile of correspondence to deal with. This may be the time to get to grips with a new computer program or some other kind of new technology. The age of the horse and cart and the quill pen are definitely over!

SUNDAY, 27TH DECEMBER
Moon square Venus

Are you sure that you aren't worrying needlessly about financial pressures in your life? Money anxieties loom large at the moment and you seem worn down by it all. Small, but irritating symptoms are undermining your health, and the root cause is stress. Try to relax and let someone else shoulder the burden for a while.

MONDAY, 28TH DECEMBER
Mercury sextile Mars

Take a discreet line when discussing money with just about everybody today – you may not want to advertise your financial position in case others try to scrounge off you! Your mind is actually working quite well now and you may come up with some kind of business idea or other money-generating scheme.

TUESDAY, 29TH DECEMBER
Saturn direct

Saturn is turning to direct motion in the area of your chart that is devoted to duties, employment and health. This suggests that if you have been struggling to get though your working days, things should go more quickly and easily from now on. You will start to receive recognition for your efforts and you may begin to feel less fatigued.

WEDNESDAY, 30TH DECEMBER
Moon trine Neptune

You may start to consider working from home now, in terms of a part-time job or a full-time, home-based career. If this is the case, there should be a very creative aspect to it because today's Neptunian aspect favours artistic ventures. A new possibility may involve a profession such as photography or making videos.

SCORPIO

THURSDAY, 31ST DECEMBER
Moon trine Mars

The stars decree a passionate encounter on this last day of the year. The Moon and Mars highlight sexuality and erotic appeal, so be prepared to be swept off your feet by sudden, intense emotions. However, if physical intimacy doesn't interest you, then anything that smacks of a mystery will. Detective books and films will be fascinating, but you could look a little closer to home because there are some financial puzzles that need sorting out too.

1999

January at a Glance

LOVE	♥			
WORK	★	★	★	
MONEY	£			
HEALTH	✪	✪	✪	
LUCK	♘	♘	♘	♘

FRIDAY, 1ST JANUARY
Mercury square Jupiter

There's only one thing worse than being wrong, and that's being right, especially when you smugly rub in your superiority. That's not the way to start off a brand new year, so stop it! An overly critical attitude will not earn you any respect. Remember that pride comes before a fall so when tables turn, as they inevitably will, you'll be the one eating humble pie.

SATURDAY, 2ND JANUARY
Full Moon

You may have to face the fact that you cannot slope off to distant and romantic shores just now. This doesn't mean that you are forever confined to your home, just that you cannot get away right now. Your mood is not only escapist but also rebellious today! You want nothing to do with people who restrict you or who remind you of your duties but you simply won't be able to escape them.

SCORPIO

SUNDAY, 3RD JANUARY
Moon opposite Venus

You aren't on top form emotionally today. In fact, your vulnerability is such that you couldn't put up any resistance to pressure or emotional blackmail now. You'd far rather follow the crowd than stand out in any way. You're very anxious to please, but this is a trait that shouldn't be taken too far. Serious decisions about the state of your relationship will have to be put off until you are feeling stronger.

MONDAY, 4TH JANUARY
Venus into Aquarius

Old scores and family squabbles can now be laid to rest as the passage of Venus into your domestic area signals a time of harmony and contentment. Surround yourself with beauty, both in terms of affection and in material possessions. This is a good time to renew a closeness with those you love. Join forces to complete a major project such as redecoration, or even a move of home itself. Be assured that the stars smile on you now.

TUESDAY, 5TH JANUARY
Venus conjunct Neptune

Home is where the heart is today and, despite the intensely romantic feeling of this day, you are best off staying in or around familiar territory. If you are in a loving relationship, now is the time to reaffirm that love and to make your feelings clear to your loved one. If you are on your own, there is a chance that you could meet someone either close to your own home or as a result of visiting other family members.

WEDNESDAY, 6TH JANUARY
Moon square Pluto

A friend is likely to put you into an embarrassing situation today because he or she may ask for a loan, and you may not want to give it. If the friend needs money, then consider a small sum that you could give without really missing it. Don't lend, give; and then forget about it. If a friend wants to borrow an item that belongs to you, then weigh up whether you are likely to get this back and then whether you need your friend or your goods the most.

THURSDAY, 7TH JANUARY
Mercury into Capricorn

Your mind will be going at full speed ahead over the next few weeks and you are bound to come up with some really great new ideas. You will be very busy with the phone ringing off its hook and letters falling into your letter box by the ton.

SCORPIO

You will find yourself acting as a temporary secretary for a while, even if the only person who makes use of your services is yourself.

FRIDAY, 8TH JANUARY
Moon trine Venus

The finer things of life have a delightful appeal today. You're in a cultured frame of mind susceptible to refined music and fine art. There's also a romantic side to this Venusian influence, so it's a time to indulge yourself in pleasure.

SATURDAY, 9TH JANUARY
Moon square Sun

You're quite introverted today. There's no doubt that you're thinking deep thoughts and getting intrigued by the most obscure facts and subjects. Don't let this pleasurable reverie distract you from the outer world though, because there's a meeting due with someone whose likely to become very special indeed.

SUNDAY, 10TH JANUARY
Moon opposite Saturn

You may not be feeling at your best today, so slow down, take some time off and coddle yourself a little. You may have the start of a cold or some kind of chronic ailment, such as backache, may come back to plague you. This isn't likely to be a wonderful day as far as work is concerned, so take a bit of time off if you can.

MONDAY, 11TH JANUARY
Moon square Uranus

Guard against accidents in the home today. If you have to clamber upwards in order to get at something, then make sure you use a proper stepladder rather than perching perilously on a rickety stool. A mother figure may say something to annoy you and, because your confidence is at rather a low ebb, you may be tempted to snap back defensively at her. This may be a good thing, who knows?

TUESDAY, 12TH JANUARY
Venus sextile Pluto

A discussion with your nearest and dearest will open your eyes to possibilities you didn't think existed. Monetarily, this will be a good thing enabling you to sort out the finances so large domestic projects can be completed to everyone's satisfaction. Your point of view will be transformed by a pooling of resources. An older relative may to contribute some cash help at this time.

SCORPIO

WEDNESDAY, 13TH JANUARY
Venus conjunct Uranus

At last, your domestic problems seem to be coming to an end. Even if there are still a few rumblings and grumblings to be heard in and around your family, the worst seems to be over. Those who have fallen out with each other will start to make up and even those who really cannot stand each other will make an effort for the time being.

THURSDAY, 14TH JANUARY
Sun sextile Jupiter

Hiding yourself indoors won't get you anywhere today, but getting out and about will bring some excellent results. You may be able to track down the job you want, find just the item you are looking for and even make a new friend or two.

FRIDAY, 15TH JANUARY
Sun square Mars

Any dealings with your neighbours or relatives are likely to be difficult today. The Sun's harsh aspect to Mars ensures that tempers will flare and certain things that should be left unsaid will come out into the open. On this of all days, discretion is definitely the better part of valour, so keep yourself to yourself as much as possible.

SATURDAY, 16TH JANUARY
Moon conjunct Mercury

You might think that you speak in a reasoned, clear voice today but your emotional intensity is showing through. You've obviously got a lot of conviction now and you can't fail to be persuasive and eloquent when you display such sincerity. If a close partnership has been going through a sticky patch, then it's time you expressed your true feelings.

SUNDAY, 17TH JANUARY
New Moon

The New Moon shows a change in your way of thinking. In many ways you'll know that it's time to move on. Perhaps you'll find yourself in a new company, a new home or among a new circle of friends in the near future. Opinions are set to change as you are influenced by more stimulating people. Perhaps you'll consider starting an educational course of some kind.

MONDAY, 18TH JANUARY
Sun square Saturn

There is no doubt about it, you are going through a difficult patch and it is

SCORPIO

extremely hard for you to get anywhere. The only thing to do is to see this as a lesson in patience and to have faith in the future. The stars do move and adverse planetary combinations don't stay that way forever. You may not be able to see a way out of your problems now, but one will turn up, sooner or later, you can bank on that.

TUESDAY, 19TH JANUARY
Moon conjunct Venus

This should be a good day for your family and your home life. Relatives may pop in with offers of help and useful gifts. Any family get-together that happens now will be extremely successful. This is a good time to buy something beautiful or valuable for your home or to arrange for refurbishment to be done. This is a good day to pick up collector's items such as antiques, *objets d'art* or good things for the home.

WEDNESDAY, 20TH JANUARY
Sun into Aquarius

The home and family become your main interest over the next four weeks as the Sun moves into the most domestic area of your chart from today. Family feuds will now be resolved, and you'll find an increasing contentment in your own surroundings. A haven of peace will be restored in your home. This should also be a period of nostalgia when happy memories come flooding back.

THURSDAY, 21ST JANUARY
Mars opposite Saturn

Other people's tendency to drag their feet could be getting you down today. On the other hand, you could be too impatient for your own good. Try to take it easy because one thing is certain.... you can't force the pace!

FRIDAY, 22ND JANUARY
Sun conjunct Neptune

This should be a very pleasant and relaxing day, and the best thing to do with it is to sprawl on the sofa with a couple of magazines, a box of chocolates to dip into and something good on the telly. If you do actually feel more energetic than this, try a visit to your local swimming baths because the feeling of being surrounded by water would be good for your nerves and even better for your aura.

SATURDAY, 23RD JANUARY
Mercury sextile Jupiter

With Mercury and Jupiter stimulating your curiosity you'll be looking for some

SCORPIO

way to stretch your mental muscles. It doesn't matter whether it's for profit or mere interest, the more you learn the better for your general state of mind. This is a day when your imagination and creative scope is at top form. You can show the world what you're really made of. Your mind is quick and perceptive and your talents are without parallel.

SUNDAY, 24TH JANUARY
Mercury square Saturn

This is going to be one of those days when you seem to take two steps forward and one backward. You may have to wait in for something important to be delivered, only to find that it doesn't arrive at all, that it has been sent to the wrong address or that it does arrive but, when you unpack it, it isn't what you ordered in the first place. You will spend the best part of the day on the phone, being given the run around by some firm which either cannot help you or whose staff don't want to know!

MONDAY, 25TH JANUARY
Moon square Uranus

You could suffer a bit of tension in or around the home today. Older family members may be making one set of demands upon you, while a partner may be making another. You cannot tear yourself in two pieces, so somebody is going to be disappointed. If you really want to set the cat among the pigeons, go out with a friend and leave them all to squabble.

TUESDAY, 26TH JANUARY
Mars into Scorpio

Mars enters your own sign of the zodiac today and it will spend a few weeks there, bringing zest, energy and a welcome element of fun into your life. You seem to be on a 'roll' at the moment and, as long as you keep up the momentum, there is no reason why you should not be able to reach your objectives.

WEDNESDAY, 27TH JANUARY
Venus sextile Saturn

You have the capacity to change and improve your environment today. Venus provides the taste and vision while Saturn ensures that you finish what you start! You could be living in a palace by this evening!

THURSDAY, 28TH JANUARY
Venus into Pisces

This is a good day to begin new projects and to get great ideas off the ground.

SCORPIO

Venus is now moving into the area of your chart that is concerned with creativity, so over the next few weeks you can take advantage of this and get involved with some kind of creative process. Venus is concerned with the production of beauty, so utilize this planetary energy to enhance any of your creations now.

FRIDAY, 29TH JANUARY
Venus trine Mars

When it comes to attractibility, there are few who could beat you at the moment. The force of your personality combines with an irresistible glamour that ensures that you'll be the centre of attraction. Your romantic interests are bound to benefit from your expression of charisma.

SATURDAY, 30TH JANUARY
Sun sextile Pluto

You may need to take some time off to do a few jobs around the home today. Anything that you do now to make the running of your home more economical will be worthwhile. If you decide to chat to your partner about his or her spending, you will find that their views are roughly the same as yours.

SUNDAY, 31ST JANUARY
Full Moon eclipse

Eclipses have had an evil reputation since the time of the Romans, but these have to occur on a particularly sensitive part of your chart for them to affect you personally. Today's little rotter will cause you some kind of unwelcome problem either at home, at work or both.

February at a Glance

LOVE	♥	♥	♥	♥	♥
WORK	★	★	★		
MONEY	£	£	£	£	
HEALTH	✚	✚	✚	✚	
LUCK	♘	♘	♘		

SCORPIO

MONDAY, 1ST FEBRUARY
Mars square Neptune

Do as little as possible today because due to the mixed influences of Neptune and Mars, anything you start will inevitable have to be done again. You could waste a lot of time if you are too determined now. Mistakes will be too easy to make.

TUESDAY, 2ND FEBRUARY
Sun conjunct Uranus

If you were expecting a peaceful day around the house, then think again! Anything could happen today! Unexpected visitors, a sudden urge to redecorate the kitchen or a disastrous dish that turns into something else. Just go with the flow and take it all as it comes!

WEDNESDAY, 3RD FEBRUARY
Sun conjunct Mercury

A good chat with a relative could open up possibilities and reveal old secrets today. The Sun meets up with Mercury in your Solar house of heritage and family issues so you'll take a great deal of pleasure in the company of those who are close to you. This should also be a time to look to the future. Perhaps a move of home should be considered now.

THURSDAY, 4TH FEBRUARY
Moon opposite Jupiter

Yet again your popularity achieves and amazing peak today. Expect to get a lot of invitations and to be the centre of attention. You may have cause for celebration now, but even if you don't, we're sure you can think of an excuse for a party. The only problem you're likely to have is to fit all these social occasions into gaps in your diary.

FRIDAY, 5TH FEBRUARY
Mercury conjunct Uranus

You are likely to be surprised by the antics of various family members today and it is your mother or your grandparents who are the most likely source of all the fun. You may hear some really unexpected news about these relatives and they may suddenly decide to descend upon your household in person in order to give you their glad tidings.

SATURDAY, 6TH FEBRUARY
Venus square Pluto

Being fond of someone is one thing, but letting your affections border on the

SCORPIO

obsessive is quite another. And that's the trend that has to be combated today for the aspect between Venus and Pluto moves your affections towards the fanatical. Try to keep a measure of common sense and you won't go far wrong, but give in to your impulses and you'll find yourself in no end of trouble.

SUNDAY, 7TH FEBRUARY
Moon conjunct Mars

A determined and businesslike attitude prevails today. Your ability to follow through on an original impulse will certainly win respect, even if you do meet a little opposition along the way. Opposition won't bother you now though. In fact, you'll relish the challenge. You can accomplish wonders now. Just one word of warning: your fiery impatience is strongly stimulated today too, so take care when driving or generally rushing about.

MONDAY, 8TH FEBRUARY
Moon square Sun

Nostalgia and more than a touch of insecurity mingle as the Moon enters a stressful aspect with the Sun today. You need some reassurance that your domestic and emotional life is safe and lasting. Any hint of change will be disturbing today so stick close to home and don't overload your schedule.

TUESDAY, 9TH FEBRUARY
Moon trine Jupiter

This should be a highly optimistic day. The Moon is in aspect to Jupiter which always lightens your mood and shows you the world from a more positive viewpoint. Your popularity is guaranteed because when you smile, everyone around you will smile too. Good humour is infectious. You've got no time for worry or boring duties. Enjoyment is the keynote of the day, and you'll be determined to make the most of it. Any dealings with children will keep you very happy indeed and make you feel youthful.

WEDNESDAY, 10TH FEBRUARY
Moon sextile Uranus

There should be a sudden and unexpected windfall for you or for some other family member. What seems certain is that if such a windfall does arrive, you will spend it on household goods or for the benefit of other family members. Don't forget to treat yourself as well. You may feel like breaking out of a rut and having a bit of freedom now, but you are actually most likely to spend any free time loafing around in or near your home.

SCORPIO

THURSDAY, 11TH FEBRUARY
Mercury sextile Saturn

The sooner you can get things straight at home and at work, the sooner you can think of having some time to yourself. However, today, it seems likely that the demands of others both at home and work will have to come first. Your efforts will be appreciated though.

FRIDAY, 12TH FEBRUARY
Mercury into Pisces

Mercury moves into a part of your horoscope that is concerned with creativity. Mercury rules such things as thinking, learning and communications, but it can also be associated with skills and craftwork of various kinds. The combination of creativity and craftwork suggests that the next few weeks would be a good time to work on hobbies such as dressmaking, carpentry and so on.

SATURDAY, 13TH FEBRUARY
Jupiter into Aries

The giant planet, Jupiter, always tends to blow things out of proportion and since it has now entered your Solar house of health, minor ailments could be far more troubling now than they were before. Digestive problems are particularly highlighted now.

SUNDAY, 14TH FEBRUARY
Moon sextile Jupiter

St Valentine's Day should be a fairly lucky one, and even though nothing spectacular is likely to happen, you should be quite happy and relaxed both among your colleagues at work and also at home with family and friends.

MONDAY, 15TH FEBRUARY
Moon conjunct Uranus

You may decide to move house! Although this may look like a spur-of-the-moment decision, it has probably been lurking at the back of your mind for a long time but you may not have felt like talking to others about this. Another possibility is that you decide to alter your present home in some dramatic way. At the very least, you will buy some large item for the home soon.

TUESDAY, 16TH FEBRUARY
New Moon eclipse

Today's eclipse urges you to look far back into your childhood for the roots of the problems that now affect you. Many guilts, hang-ups and inhibitions remain

SCORPIO

from that time, and it's the perfect opportunity to rid yourself of these adolescent encumbrances. Recent events have forced you to question your place in a family or home that seems stifling and out of tune with your inner self. Today's events should help you make more sense out of the situation.

WEDNESDAY, 17TH FEBRUARY
Sun sextile Saturn

Your mood is likely to be serious and you are not about to put up with any nonsense today. You may work very hard now either on a home-based project or on something that really needs to be done for long-term benefit at an office or factory.

THURSDAY, 18TH FEBRUARY
Mercury square Pluto

Money matters are your main source of concern today. Though your worries are over minor expenses, to you they have achieved major proportions. In the long run, most of your anxieties will be groundless but at the moment they are very pressing indeed. Try to calm down, and if it makes you feel better, try to sort out a sensible budget. You may not stick to it, but you'll feel justified in making the effort. If you're a gambling sort, I should resist the impulse for today at least.

FRIDAY, 19TH FEBRUARY
Sun into Pisces

You are going to be in a slightly frivolous frame of mind over the next few weeks and you shouldn't punish yourself for this. Pay attention to a creative interest or a demanding hobby now or get involved in something creative on behalf of others. A couple of typical examples would be to be the production of a school play or making preparations for a flower and vegetable show.

SATURDAY, 20TH FEBRUARY
Void Moon

This is one of those days when none of the planets is making any worthwhile kind of aspect to any of the others. Even the Moon is 'void of course', which means that it is not making any aspects of any importance to any of the other planets. On such a day, avoid starting anything new and don't set out to do anything important. Do what needs to be done and take some time off for a rest.

SUNDAY, 21ST FEBRUARY
Venus into Aries

Venus moves out of the fun, sun and pleasure area of your chart into the work,

SCORPIO

duty and health area, and it will stay there for the next few weeks. This suggests that any problems related to work and duty will become easier to handle and also that you could start to see some kind of practical outcome from all that you have been doing lately. If you have been off-colour recently, Venus will help you to feel better soon.

MONDAY, 22ND FEBRUARY
Venus sextile Neptune

You may have some kind of inspired idea which helps you to find an easy way through an awkward problem. A friend may help out at work or at home and, in addition to this, any help that you give others will be greatly appreciated. Take the opportunity to listen to music, read a romantic story or enjoy looking at something beautiful today because you seem to need this kind of mental refreshment and inspiration.

TUESDAY, 23RD FEBRUARY
Moon opposite Pluto

Guard against being talked into buying anything today. Avoid slick salesmen (or women) like the plague and don't agree to anything on the phone or on the doorstep in order to get the vendor off your back. You need to think carefully about any kind of joint agreement or business matter, but you must avoid being rail-roaded into anything that is against your own interests.

WEDNESDAY, 24TH FEBRUARY
Venus conjunct Jupiter

You are definitely reviewing your work situation and today there will be a golden opportunity to do something about this. You may be offered a great new job now or you may be given some belated recognition for the work that you have done in the past. You may receive some kind of bonus or commission soon too.

THURSDAY, 25TH FEBRUARY
Moon trine Sun

If you have friends, relatives or even work connections that are overseas or at a distance from you, you could hear from these today. There seems to be good things coming to you from afar, thus invitations, opportunities and the chance of a bit of fun in connection with travel could be on the way now.

FRIDAY, 26TH FEBRUARY
Sun trine Mars

A passionate outlook today, with you exuding a magnetic aura that will prove

SCORPIO

irresistible. A forthright manner will win a lot of flattery and true admiration. If you are interested in sport, then a more active participation is encouraged too.

SATURDAY, 27TH FEBRUARY
Jupiter sextile Neptune

If you've ever craved the home of your dreams, today's combination of Jupiter and Neptune could just make that wish come true. Some will be lucky enough to receive a windfall making domestic improvements possible.

SUNDAY, 28TH FEBRUARY
Moon opposite Uranus

A sudden and unexpected event could send you scurrying home from work in order to sort out a domestic crisis. Alternatively, you may not be able to get home at your usual time due to a crisis at your place of work. One of your superiors could be shunted out of his or her job, leaving a mass of work entirely in your hands. If this is the case, you may find that your family are less than sympathetic with your plight.

March at a Glance

LOVE	♥	♥	♥	♥	
WORK	★				
MONEY	£	£	£		
HEALTH	✪	✪			
LUCK	☘	☘	☘	☘	☘

MONDAY, 1ST MARCH
Saturn into Taurus

Saturn enters your seventh Solar house of relationships with others today and it will reside there for the next couple of years or so. You may become involved in a working partnership during this time or you may marry and take on family responsibilities soon.

SCORPIO

TUESDAY, 2ND MARCH
Mercury into Aries

The movement of Mercury into your Solar sixth house of work, duties and health suggests that a slightly more serious phase is on the way. Over the next three weeks or so you will have to concentrate on what needs to be done rather than on having a good time. You may have a fair bit to do with neighbours, colleagues and relatives of around your own age group soon and you will have to spend a fair bit of time on the phone to them.

WEDNESDAY, 3RD MARCH
Venus trine Pluto

Those of you who are alone and who want to meet someone should keep your eyes open at work. Another good place to look for love would be your local garden centre, an art gallery or anywhere connected with music! This may sound crazy but the idea is that anywhere that deals in goods that appeal to the senses could have a romantic attachment for you now.

THURSDAY, 4TH MARCH
Venus sextile Uranus

If you find yourself up to your neck in chores and unable to cope with them all, see if a friend or one of your parents can help you out. You seem to be stuck with the boring jobs although everything inside you is crying out for freedom and a change of scene at the moment.

FRIDAY, 5TH MARCH
Mercury sextile Neptune

You will be able to zip through the chores at home today and, if you are home-based, you will be able to get out and about sooner than usual. This is a good time to buy or mend something that uses water or something that involves the use of fluids. This could mean replacing a washing machine or a dishwasher now or buying something amusing, such as a yoghurt-maker.

SATURDAY, 6TH MARCH
Moon square Neptune

Something has come back from the past to haunt you. You may literally be experiencing strange psychic phenomena and things that go bump in the night, but it is probably more likely that your own past seems to be coming back at you in a rather depressing or unusual way.

SCORPIO

SUNDAY, 7TH MARCH
Moon square Uranus

This is one of those days when something could go unexpectedly wrong. You may have to leave what you are doing in order to sort out a family problem or to pour oil on troubled family waters. A friend may come round to your home later on, needing a shoulder to cry upon and a listening ear.

MONDAY, 8TH MARCH
Moon trine Venus

An office romance or a chance meeting at work which turns into love is quite possible from today onwards! Even if this is not the case, you could enjoy a gentle flirtation with the delivery girl or the man who calls round to your workplace. There should be goodwill and kindness around you both at work and among any people whom you work with in a voluntary capacity.

TUESDAY, 9TH MARCH
Moon trine Jupiter

You have the leisure to take some time to look at the financial realities of your life today. Though the picture may not be as bright as you'd wish, you'll soon see that improvements can be made. I'm not just talking about budgeting here; you may have been thinking about a new post which would be more lucrative. If so, you'll make up your mind to take it now.

WEDNESDAY, 10TH MARCH
Mercury retrograde

Everything comes to a dead stop in your working environment as Mercury again pauses in his course. News of opportunities may now be delayed. Letters, phone calls and professional contacts are either mistimed or full of evasion. Don't worry, this period will pass, but you'll have to put up with it until 14th October.

THURSDAY, 11TH MARCH
Moon square Mercury

It's a very tense outlook today for the Moon and Mercury put your nerves on edge. Of course, your own anxieties will prove to be far more exhausting than any outside influence in your life just now. If you're wise, you'll avoid challenges today and indulge in some relaxation. If you do insist on facing up to every little thing that the world throws at you, you'll end up depleted and glum.

SCORPIO

FRIDAY, 12TH MARCH
Moon sextile Mars

You will tend to talk nineteen to the dozen today. In fact the power of your personality expressed through your speech will be devastating and you could sweep all opposition away with forceful argument.

SATURDAY, 13TH MARCH
Mercury sextile Neptune

You may start the day with the uncomfortable realization that your home isn't exactly how you'd like it to be! Fortunately, Mercury and Neptune team up to give you imagination enough to see what you can make it. We hope your energy levels are on the up because there's work to be done!

SUNDAY, 14TH MARCH
Moon sextile Pluto

This is a good day to buy something for the home and it would be better still if you can take your partner with you so that you do the choosing together. If you don't want to spend too much money just now, you may find ways of recycling goods that you have used before. You may even be able to pick up a real bargain at a jumble sale or a second-hand shop. (Our American readers should try scouring the thrift shops and the pre-owned shops!)

MONDAY, 15TH MARCH
Moon sextile Venus

They say that the good things in life are free. Though you may have doubts on that score, you're convinced that life's not worth living unless you're enjoying yourself. The only trouble with that is that you'll be inclined to over-indulge today. Good food and wines are for gourmets, so make sure that you aren't a glutton! Otherwise, you'll regret your woeful physical state tomorrow.

TUESDAY, 16TH MARCH
Moon square Pluto

Guard against losing anything today. If you have valuable jewellery or other goods that cost good money, then leave them at home and don't risk the chance of them being stolen. Be careful not to mislay something and be especially careful when in the garden, at a playing field or anywhere else in the open air because the earth itself may decide to claim your goods today!

SCORPIO

WEDNESDAY, 17TH MARCH
New Moon

There's a New Moon today casting a glow over your artistic potential. Your talents should shine now so have some belief in yourself and in what you can offer to the world at large. If art and literature leave you cold, you may be more inclined to an amorous path. Conventional values are not for you now since you're determined to be yourself and to chart your own course. Make time to have fun, you deserve it.

THURSDAY, 18TH MARCH
Venus into Taurus

Venus, the planet of romance, moves into your horoscope area of close relationships from today increasing your physical desires and bringing the light of love into your heart. If you're involved in a long-term partnership it's a chance to renew the magic of the early days of your union. If single, then the next few weeks should bring a stunning new attraction into your life.

FRIDAY, 19TH MARCH
Sun conjunct Mercury

Communication is the name of the game today as this will enhance all your relationships. You could have a really enjoyable chat to a friend or you could sit and talk things over with your lover today. You may decide to start a creative venture now and, if so, this is the time to do some research on your ideas and to see what materials and methods would best suit your purpose.

SATURDAY, 20TH MARCH
Venus conjunct Saturn

Love and romance are all very well but the practicalities of your relationship needs to be looked at too. You may decide that you need to save up a bit more money before you and your lover can splurge on the kind of things that you really want.

SUNDAY, 21ST MARCH
Sun into Aries

The Sun moves into your Solar sixth house of work and duty for the next month. This Solar movement will also encourage you to concentrate on your health and well-being and also that of your family. If you are off-colour, the Sun will help you to get back to full health once again. If you have jobs that need to be done, the next month or so will be a good time to get them done.

SCORPIO

MONDAY, 22ND MARCH
Moon trine Neptune

You may start to consider working from home now, either in some kind of part-time pin-money job or even in a fully blown home-based career. If this is the case, there would have to be a very creative aspect to this because today's Neptune aspect would make it easy to get creative projects off the ground now. A possibility that you may not have thought of would involve something like photography or the making of videos.

TUESDAY, 23RD MARCH
Venus square Neptune

You may harbour some nasty suspicions about your partner now. Don't make your mind up about what you think he or she may be doing until you have real evidence of underhandedness or wrongdoing.

WEDNESDAY, 24TH MARCH
Moon square Sun

Though you have the promise of high achievement coming up, it's important that you don't overload your schedule or take on far more than you can comfortably cope with. It's very tempting to push hard now, but watch out for the law of diminishing returns. The more you take on, the more tired you'll be and the harder the effort needed to complete your tasks. Be easy on yourself; everything is going well so coast along with it. You don't need to store up stressful problems for the future.

THURSDAY, 25TH MARCH
Sun sextile Neptune

A lovely aspect between the Sun and Neptune puts you in a romantic frame of mind. Unfortunately, it doesn't look as if life and circumstances are going to allow you to pursue your dreams today.

FRIDAY, 26TH MARCH
Moon square Saturn

While one set of people think that you are definitely the best thing since sliced bread, another set seem to think that you are a lot less than perfect. If you habitually rely upon the opinions of others in order to judge your own worth, this situation will make you very confused. Work out your own assessment of yourself and don't listen to others.

SCORPIO

SATURDAY, 27TH MARCH
Venus opposite Mars

Today is much like the irresistible force meeting the immovable object – something's got to give, but not just yet! At least it's all going to be out in the open and you will know what you have to deal with.

SUNDAY, 28TH MARCH
Void Moon

Occasionally one finds a day in which neither the planets nor the Moon make any major aspects to each other, and on such a day the Moon's course is said to be 'void'. There is nothing wrong with a day like this but there is no point in trying to start anything new or anything important because there isn't enough of a planetary boost to get it off the ground. Stick to your normal routine.

MONDAY, 29TH MARCH
Moon square Pluto

You feel the need to keep some control over your finances now but your friends are encouraging you to go out and spend money like water. You may do a bit of both today.

TUESDAY, 30TH MARCH
Jupiter trine Pluto

Big money coming your way is a possibility today as Jupiter and Pluto join up to repay you for all the hard work you've put in the past! Worries should now be eased as both your working life and your health concerns look more positive for the future.

WEDNESDAY, 31ST MARCH
Full Moon

Apart from a slightly frustrating full Moon situation today, there is not much going on in the planetary firmament. The best thing to do is to stick to your usual way of doing things and to avoid starting anything new or important. If you feel off-colour or out of sorts, then take whatever medicines you need and try not to work too hard.

SCORPIO

April at a Glance

LOVE	♥	♥	♥	♥
WORK	★	★	★	
MONEY	£	£		
HEALTH	☉	☉	☉	☉
LUCK	♘	♘	♘	

THURSDAY, 1ST APRIL
Sun conjunct Jupiter

A wonderful aspect between the Sun and Jupiter suggests that this should be a real red-letter day! You should hear the news you want and, whether this be a tremendous opportunity of some kind or a chance to get your hands on some real money, you should go for it with all your might. Those of you who love animals could have a very pleasant surprise now; perhaps someone will make you a gift of a fluffy little kitten or a simply wonderful puppy.

FRIDAY, 2ND APRIL
Mercury direct

You should try to stretch your mind by pitting your wits against a problem or two now. There is no need for this to be a serious matter; it may simply be a case of doing a couple of crosswords, enjoying a game of chess or Scrabble, or doing something more energetic, such as enjoying a game of snooker or badminton with a friend.

SATURDAY, 3RD APRIL
Moon conjunct Mars

This will bring a rush of blood to you head! Well, it will if you try standing on your head, won't it? And that's just one of the crazy things you might do today! Your emotions will be close to the surface. You may feel terribly angry or perhaps suffering from what psychologists call 'free-floating anxiety'. Although there appears to be no real reason for this on the surface, the cause is a combination of many things that have been piling up on you over the last few weeks.

SCORPIO

SUNDAY, 4TH APRIL
Mercury sextile Venus
Your mind and heart seem to be in harmony with each other now. Feelings of loneliness and abandonment will vanish, and you will feel more loved and cherished than you have for a long time past.

MONDAY, 5TH APRIL
Moon sextile Neptune
You could go completely overboard today! Your mood is very excitable and pretty strange too! You could easily fall in love with an object that you simply must have no matter what the cost! Try to hold back until you can look at the item with less passion.

TUESDAY, 6TH APRIL
Saturn square Neptune
Your get up and go, looks as though it's got up and gone today as the gloomy planet Saturn gets a grip on your sex life! To put it mildly, things will not go too well. On the other hand, this is a temporary blip and will soon pass. Try not to get too oversensitive about it.

WEDNESDAY, 7TH APRIL
Sun sextile Uranus
You can now begin to make sense of both your home and your work situation and friends may come up with solutions for problems in both of these areas of your life. You may be given an opportunity to buy something for the home at a real knock-down price and your parental figures may come up with ways and means of getting this from where it is to where you want it to go.

THURSDAY, 8TH APRIL
Moon sextile Mars
If there's any campaign around that needs a good spokesperson, then they need look no further than you. You've got all the energy, enthusiasm and determination to stand up for the rights of others. Of course, to get you to stand on a soapbox, someone has to catch you first, and that's no easy task since you'll be racing around your neighbourhood trying to get a million things done at once. Hasn't it ever occurred to you to slow down at all?

FRIDAY, 9TH APRIL
Moon sextile Mercury
This could be a red-letter day! Letters, phone calls and faxes could bring you great

SCORPIO

news. It might be worth making a small bet on something or other today because the planets seem to indicate some kind of windfall. This doesn't mean that you should put a large sum of money down on a wager because the planets are not that infallible. However, it may be worthwhile taking a chance with a very small amount.

SATURDAY, 10TH APRIL
Moon square Saturn

Though your mood is rather carefree, the same can't be said for either your partner or your family in general. Everyone in your close circle seems worried and pessimistic now and you'll have to make efforts not to fall into their gloomy trap. However, no amount of encouragement from you will break this sombre mood so avoid contact for a while and allow people to resume an even keel on their own.

SUNDAY, 11TH APRIL
Moon sextile Sun

If you need to get through some chores in and around your home, this is a good day to do so. Do-it-yourself jobs, tidying up, cooking, cleaning and gardening will all go well and make you feel that you have had a really useful day.

MONDAY, 12TH APRIL
Venus into Gemini

Venus enters the area of your chart that is closely involved with love and sex today. Oddly enough, this aspect can bring the end of a difficult relationship or, just as easily begin a wonderful new one. If you have been dating but haven't got around to 'mating', this could be the start of something wonderful. Your emotional life over the next two or three weeks should be something to remember, that's for sure!

TUESDAY, 13TH APRIL
Moon sextile Venus

It's a day of relaxation, but not necessarily of calm. The Lunar aspect of Venus puts you in a sensual mood, determined to enjoy the finer things of life. Good food, good wines and the company of someone you love are the recipe for perfect bliss. It doesn't matter what you do, as long as you enjoy it. Give yourself over to absolute pleasure today.

WEDNESDAY, 14TH APRIL
Moon into Aries

It would be worth concentrating on getting the chores done today because the chances are that you will be very busy over the next few weeks. Get the ironing done, wash the car, mend that leaking tap and sort out your paperwork. You will feel terribly pleased with yourself for having got these jobs done and out of the way. When you have done all this, sit down and pour yourself a liberal tot of your favourite brew.

THURSDAY, 15TH APRIL
Moon conjunct Jupiter

In matters of health you should be feeling pretty good. Even if you've been suffering from the effects of over-indulgence, the outlook shows a that you're on the mend. Working affairs too benefit from the Lunar conjunction with Jupiter bringing a breadth of vision and plenty of opportunities for advancement. Connections with foreign countries are emphasized. If you're looking for work, then broaden your horizons because there is unexpected opportunity just waiting for you.

FRIDAY, 16TH APRIL
New Moon

Today's New Moon gives you the stamina to shrug off any minor ailments that have been troubling you. Occurring, as it does, in your Solar house of health and work, it's obvious that you need to get yourself into shape to face the challenges that await you. A few early nights, a better diet and a readiness to give up bad habits such as smoking, will work wonders.

SATURDAY, 17TH APRIL
Mercury into Aries

Some monetary worries should be alleviated by Mercury's change of sign today. Of course, this does not come without effort and you may find that you have to take on a part-time job in the short term to get the books to balance. More generally, improvements in the job stakes are now possible, but you'll have to be keenly aware of the possible competition and prepared to act instantly to get the employment you want.

SUNDAY, 18TH APRIL
Moon conjunct Venus

This should be an intensely passionate time as the influence on Venus is triggered by the conjunction with the Moon. Your sex life is due to be boosted in a most delightful way. Apart from the physical advantages of the conjunction it also works to your economic advantage. Contracts and financial agreements are bound to work in your favour.

SCORPIO

MONDAY, 19TH APRIL
Mars opposite Saturn

The path of true love rarely runs completely smoothly and today is one of those days where there are stones and obstacles placed on your road. Your lover may be too busy working to spend much time with you or, alternatively, both of you have family responsibilities that are getting in the way of your relationship. This will soon pass.

TUESDAY, 20TH APRIL
Sun into Taurus

The Sun moves into the area of your chart devoted to relationships from today. If things have been difficult in a partnership, either personal or in business, then this is your chance to put everything back into its proper place. It's obvious that the significant other in your life deserves respect and affection and that's just what you're now prepared to give. Teamwork is the key to success over the next month.

WEDNESDAY, 21ST APRIL
Venus opposite Pluto

You may find it hard to express your feelings to the one you love today. It is possible that you could try to sort out a number of financial or practical difficulties between you and your lover now, only to find that he or she walks away from you and does not want to listen to what you have to say.

THURSDAY, 22ND APRIL
Mercury sextile Neptune

Imagination combines with considerable brain-power today so that should sort out any problem that comes your way. You will be intuitively in touch with the feelings of family members and work colleagues.

FRIDAY, 23RD APRIL
Jupiter sextile Uranus

You could get a sudden desire to move home today. Either that or you'll want some major changes to the one you are in! The combination of Jupiter and Uranus shows rapid movement and the desire for change, so don't hang around…get to it!

SATURDAY, 24TH APRIL
Sun opposite Mars

Any harsh aspect between the Sun and Mars warns against impulsive actions.

SCORPIO

These two fiery planets urge you into an aggressive mode that's too hot to handle. Any relationship difficulties will erupt into a furious quarrel if you don't exercise self-control today. Tempers are too quick for comfort, so try to slow down and to think before you react!

SUNDAY, 25TH APRIL
Moon trine Saturn

You seem to be making some quite important long-term decisions now and the indications are that this is the right thing to do. Some of these decisions revolve around partnerships or relationships and they could in time lead you either into or out of some kind of major commitment.

MONDAY, 26TH APRIL
Mercury trine Pluto

Someone seems to have been working behind the scenes to improve your financial position. If you have been relying upon others to pay your way recently, it looks as though you will soon be able to contribute more to the household (or business) coffers yourself.

TUESDAY, 27TH APRIL
Sun conjunct Saturn

The conjunction between the Sun and Saturn today mark a new and rather responsible attitude to relationships on your part. Your lover could also decide to take things further and to deepen his or her feelings for you from now on. Although this transit only lasts for a day, its effects could last for months to come, so it is an important one.

WEDNESDAY, 28TH APRIL
Moon opposite Mercury

If you are engaged in a long and detailed task such as dressmaking, do-it-yourself or craftwork of some other kind, you may find the going difficult today. You may encounter unexpected difficulties in your task or you may have to set the whole job aside in order to do something more important for a while. Work of all kinds could be frustrating for at least part of the day today.

THURSDAY, 29TH APRIL
Mercury sextile Uranus

There may be an unexpected breakthrough for you in your job situation soon. If, for example, you have been looking for the right job for some time, it could suddenly drop into your lap now.

SCORPIO

FRIDAY, 30TH APRIL
Full Moon

The Full Moon in your sign shows that you've come to the end of a personal phase and that it's time to tie up the loose ends and move on. This should be an opportunity to rid yourself of harmful little habits and create a whole new persona. This could be an image transformation. So, if you're at all dissatisfied by the way you present yourself to the world, then work out your own personal make-over. You'll be astounded by the reception the new you gets.

May at a Glance

LOVE	❤	❤	❤	❤	❤
WORK	★	★			
MONEY	£	£	£	£	
HEALTH	✛				
LUCK	U	U			

SATURDAY, 1ST MAY
Mercury conjunct Jupiter

This is a great day in which to improve your working situation so, if you are out of work, look for something good today. Those of you who are already settled in a job could receive some special recognition today for the work that you have completed over the past few months. Even if you only work at home or in your garden, you will be pleased with your efforts today.

SUNDAY, 2ND MAY
Moon sextile Neptune

You'll be strangely excitable today. The Lunar aspect to Neptune makes you too ready to splash out the cash and to purchase anything pretty that takes your eye. In small matters this will do no harm but think twice before committing yourself to major expense.

MONDAY, 3RD MAY
Moon sextile Uranus

You will have a very clever money-making idea today and, whether this makes you

SCORPIO

a fortune or simply brings in a small but useful sum, it will be worthwhile. You could stumble across something that looks like a broken piece of junk in a jumble sale or a car boot sale, only to find on closer inspection that it is either something quirky but useful to your present circumstances, or even that it is highly valuable.

TUESDAY, 4TH MAY
Moon opposite Venus

You may want to be the last of the big spenders today but it is not really a good idea. You may need to consult an accountant or your bank manager in order to see what you can or cannot get away with during the months ahead. There is no doubt about it, whether you have only yourself to answer to or whether you are part of any kind of partnership, you will have to cut down on the luxuries for a while.

WEDNESDAY, 5TH MAY
Mars into Libra

You seem to be entering a placid and peaceful backwater just now because Mars is disappearing into the quietest area of your chart. However, this is not quite true because you will spend this reflective time working out what you want from life and also making preparations for your future. This is a good time to repay any loans or to fulfil any outstanding obligations towards others.

THURSDAY, 6TH MAY
Moon square Jupiter

You're too easily persuaded today, so try to keep your tongue in your cheek when you are encouraged in a course of action that you know deep down is not for you. There's plenty of optimism about but most of it is misplaced. Let caution be your watchword today, and if you are at all in doubt, then do nothing!

FRIDAY, 7TH MAY
Neptune retrograde

The large, distant and slow-moving planet, Neptune, turns to retrograde motion today. This will bring a slowdown of affairs related to your home, family and domestic circumstances. You may have some kind of long-running problem regarding older female friends and relatives over the next few months too.

SATURDAY, 8TH MAY
Mercury into Taurus

The inquisitive Mercury moves into your Solar house of marriage and long-lasting relationships from today ushering in a period when a renewed understanding can be reached between yourself and your partner. New relationships can be formed

SCORPIO

under this influence too, though these will tend to be on a light, fairly superficial level. Good humour and plenty of charm should be a feature for a few weeks, though you must try to curb a tendency to needlessly criticize another's foibles. Remember, not even you are perfect!

SUNDAY, 9TH MAY
Mercury sextile Venus

You can charm the birds out of the trees today because your ability to be tactful and diplomatic are at an all-time high. If you feel like bit of company, call up a friend or a relative and have a chat.

MONDAY, 10TH MAY
Moon square Pluto

Younger members of the family may cause some kind of problem today and they could turn the home into a temporary battlefield. You may feel that one of your children is being manipulated by an older, stronger and less scrupulous youngster from elsewhere. You yourself could find your ideas being challenged in some kind of manipulative or unpleasant manner today.

TUESDAY, 11TH MAY
Mercury square Neptune

Your subconscious mind is bubbling away today. The combination of Mercury, planet of rationality, and Neptune, planet of imagination, ensures that the slightest thing will either make you unrealistically optimistic or conversely full of dread. Reality doesn't seem to get much of a look-in today!

WEDNESDAY, 12TH MAY
Moon trine Pluto

If you have recently lost or mislaid anything, it should turn up again today. The same mysterious force that took your possessions away from you will operate in the other direction today, by just as mysteriously returning them! You should receive good news about work and also about any health matters that have been bothering you recently.

THURSDAY, 13TH MAY
Mercury conjunct Saturn

This is an excellent day to sit down and talk things over with any kind of partner or associate. This may mean having a family conference with the husband or the wife or a business meeting with a working associate. If you are arranging some kind of fund-raising event, then this too will need a bit of joint planning today.

SCORPIO

FRIDAY, 14TH MAY
Moon sextile Venus

The love life is emphasized under the marvellous aspect between the Moon and Venus. This could be the start of a new and very important relationship or just a renewal of ties that have become a matter of habit. The bonds of affection and attraction are very strong. Expressions of love will be easily and sincerely made now. The more creative souls are particularly favoured under such fortunate stars.

SATURDAY, 15TH MAY
New Moon

The only planetary activity today is a New Moon in your opposite sign. It is possible that this could bring the start of a new relationship for the lonely but, to be honest, this planetary aspect is a bit too weak for such a big event. It is much more likely that you will improve on a current relationship rather than start a new one at this time.

SUNDAY, 16TH MAY
Venus sextile Saturn

There is a pleasant atmosphere around you at the moment and your inner thoughts and feelings seem to be in harmony with those of other people. A relationship seems to be going in the right direction now and there is a feeling of strength and stability in the way you and your partner feel about each other. A man in a position of authority may show you how to improve your outlook on life.

MONDAY, 17TH MAY
Mercury square Uranus

An irritable atmosphere prevails around the home today, and though you may not be aware of it you are as much to blame as your partner. To avoid any further unpleasantness, try to restrain your tongue. A tactless remark could have unforeseen consequences!

TUESDAY, 18TH MAY
Moon sextile Saturn

You have the ability to impress others today and you will earn the respect of those who matter. You may be seen as the 'elder statesman' of your group, even if you happen to be both young and/or female.

WEDNESDAY, 19TH MAY
Moon square Jupiter

This is not the best time to make any kind of travel plans and if you have a journey

SCORPIO

to make, it will be subject to delays and difficulties of various kinds. Even plans for future travel are likely to be frustrating and disappointing, so leave all this if you can until a later date. You may be waiting to hear from someone overseas and this news too will be delayed or slightly upsetting in some way.

THURSDAY, 20TH MAY
Moon opposite Neptune

Watch out for skulduggery in your place of work today. What you see may not be what you get and what you are told may be far from the truth of the matter. If you have to leave the children unattended at home for any reason, make sure that they and the house are safe. If you are not happy about this, then get someone in to take care of them or take them with you, just to be on the safe side.

FRIDAY, 21ST MAY
Sun into Gemini

Today, the Sun enters your Solar eighth house of beginnings and endings. Thus, over the next month, you can expect something to wind its way to a conclusion, while something else starts to take its place. This doesn't seem to signify a major turning point or any really big event in your life, but it does mark one of those small turning points that we all go through from time to time.

SATURDAY, 22ND MAY
Uranus retrograde

Your own surroundings hold little appeal as the erratic Uranus begins a retrograde course today. You're afflicted by wanderlust but for one reason or another can't quite get organized enough to do anything about it. If you aren't careful, this restless attitude could come over as rebellion as you reject what you know in favour of the new and exciting. Patience may be a dirty word to you, yet you'd be wise to exercise some, especially since this mood will soon pass and you'll be left with a resentful family unit.

SUNDAY, 23RD MAY
Mercury into Gemini

Mercury moves into one of the most sensitive areas of your chart from today. Anything of an intimate nature from your physical relationships to the state of your bank balance comes under scrutiny now. Turn your heightened perceptions to your love life, important partnerships, and any affair that deals with investment, insurance, tax or shared resources. An intelligent approach now will save you a lot of problems later.

SCORPIO

MONDAY, 24TH MAY
Moon trine Mercury

Rely on your instincts today because they won't let you down. Sometimes the unconscious mind urges you in directions that the conscious ego wouldn't consider. Today you're are at your intuitive best. You'll be able to detect the most subtle signals of the moods and true thoughts of those around you. This is an almost psychic influence that you'd do well to heed.

TUESDAY, 25TH MAY
Sun trine Neptune

You may be in something of a dreamy mood today, and the chances are that you will have your mind on your house or some other property that you own or that you have to deal with. You may be dreaming about improving the place or buying new carpets and furniture to make it look better. We hope your dreams come true.

WEDNESDAY, 26TH MAY
Sun conjunct Mercury

Approach contracts and agreements with caution today. That's not to say that they are bad things to get involved with, just that you've got to play your cards close to your chest to make the most of them. You have the ability to handle any negotiations with ease since your shrewd appreciation of realities gives you the edge over any opponents. You'll have no trouble with small print.

THURSDAY, 27TH MAY
Moon square Neptune

There is something funny going on in your family circle at the moment and it is hard for you to work out exactly what it is. It may be some time before all this becomes completely clear.

FRIDAY, 28TH MAY
Moon square Uranus

The planets spell danger for everyone today, so please take extra care when cooking or handling dangerous tools. After you have finished what you are doing at home, at work, in the garden or on the farm, be sure to put everything away safely and to make sure that all fires are properly dowsed.

SATURDAY, 29TH MAY
Mars opposite Jupiter

This is not the luckiest of days so don't take any chances and don't gamble on

SCORPIO

anything. Keep your money in your pocket and your mouth firmly shut. You may not be able to avoid every form of trouble but you can at least avoid making any more than necessary.

SUNDAY, 30TH MAY
Full Moon

Today's full Moon seems to be highlighting a minor problem in connection with financial matters today. You may have been overspending recently and this could be the cause of your current financial embarrassment, but there does seem to be something deeper to be considered here. Perhaps the firm you work for has a temporary problem or maybe your partner is a bit short of cash just now.

MONDAY, 31ST MAY
Venus square Mars

Venus in a horoscope represents females (among many other things) while Mars represents males (among many other things). When these two planets are ninety degrees apart, this causes tension between the sexes. Therefore, today, you may be faced with a rabid 'woman's libber' or a true 'male chauvinist pig' of the old-fashioned kind. There is no point in arguing with such people; they are too full of their own opinions (and their own egos) to listen.

June at a Glance

LOVE	♥			
WORK	★	★	★	
MONEY	£	£	£	
HEALTH	✚	✚	✚	✚
LUCK	⋃	⋃	⋃	

TUESDAY, 1ST JUNE
Venus square Jupiter

If you have expenses in connection with work, remember to claim them before they are forgotten. If any such claims are likely to be disputed, make sure you have receipts to cover all eventualities.

SCORPIO

WEDNESDAY, 2ND JUNE
Sun opposite Pluto

You are being plagued with joint financial problems. It may be a good idea to review the way you and your partner deal with money and then work out what to do for the best. You may have a business partner who is not dealing fairly with you and it is also possible that you are the one who is not dealing quite fairly with others.

THURSDAY, 3RD JUNE
Mars direct

Mars is turning to direct motion today and this is likely to affect your thinking and your planning for the future. This is a good time to repay debts and to clear the slate of any obligations that you owe others. You may find that you are doing much for others and leaving your own needs aside for a while, but this needs to be done before you can concentrate on yourself once again.

FRIDAY, 4TH JUNE
Mercury trine Mars

Even though you'll have the impulse to confide in someone you trust, restrain it today. Secrets are there to be kept and you'd better keep anything connected with your sex life and personal finances under your hat.

SATURDAY, 5TH JUNE
Venus into Leo

Venus moves into your Solar house of ambition and prominence from today. If you're involved in any career in the arts, beautification, entertainment or public relations, then you're bound to do well over the next few weeks. Those who work for women bosses won't do badly either since a female influence in the workplace will aid their ambitions. Since Venus is the planet of charisma use diplomacy to solve professional problems. You can hardly fail to win with such a capacity for charm.

SUNDAY, 6TH JUNE
Moon square Pluto

If you are engaged on a creative project, you may find that you have to shelve it for the time being. Perhaps the money has temporarily run out or maybe other people are unable to help you reach your goals. There may not be enough time or energy to complete the task, so it will have to be left until things change for the better.

SCORPIO

MONDAY, 7TH JUNE
Mercury into Cancer

Mercury enters your Solar house of adventure on philosophy from today and stimulates your curiosity. Everything from international affairs to religious questions will tax your mind. Your desire to travel will be boosted for a few weeks, as indeed will a need to expand your knowledge, perhaps by taking up a course at a local college. Keep an open mind. Allow yourself encounters with new ideas.

TUESDAY, 8TH JUNE
Sun trine Uranus

Financially, today's events should be very beneficial. Some will receive a windfall, while others could benefit from an insurance or endowment policy maturing. Whatever the reason, you may as well have an impromptu celebration at home to mark the occasion.

WEDNESDAY, 9TH JUNE
Moon sextile Uranus

A friend may come up with a solution to some of your problems. He or she will suggest easier ways of doing things either at home or at work, or both. He or she could suggest a quite imaginative or revolutionary way of tackling things that you wouldn't have thought of. It is not that you are stupid; it is simply that you are too close to the situation to be able to see it clearly.

THURSDAY, 10TH JUNE
Venus opposite Neptune

All your good intentions will come to nothing today. You are the soul of kindness, filled with nothing but good intentions, but these will either be completely misunderstood or they will misfire. Women in particular will be uncooperative and unwilling to be helped or understood. A friend may wear you out by crying on your shoulder about his or her problems and, although you try to do your best, it looks as though they don't actually want to be helped, other than to be allowed to wallow in their unhappiness.

FRIDAY, 11TH JUNE
Moon square Uranus

If you are a solo operator and would like to become a part of a couple, then do take things easily today because if you are too eager, you may frighten a potential lover away. Nobody likes to think that they are simply filling a gap; we all want to be loved irresistibly just for who we are and not simply because someone else needs a partner.

SCORPIO

SATURDAY, 12TH JUNE
Moon trine Neptune

If you have any kind of joint financial venture on the go at the moment, this will start to do rather well now. A partner or lover's finances will pick up and this will have a knock-on effect on your life and your plans together. You may, for example, start to make plans for a new home together.

SUNDAY, 13TH JUNE
New Moon

Apart from a New Moon today, there are no major planetary happenings. This suggests that you avoid making major changes in your life just now but make a couple of fresh starts in very minor matters. You may feel like taking your partner to task over his or her irritating ways, but perhaps today is not the best day for doing this.

MONDAY, 14TH JUNE
Venus trine Pluto

A woman may be instrumental in helping you solve a money or a business problem of some kind. This woman may not be a specialist in your own particular sphere but her sound common-sense ideas will help you to see your situation more clearly. If you do decide to consult a financial specialist, you will get some useful advice now.

TUESDAY, 15TH JUNE
Mercury sextile Saturn

If you need to deal with legal or official matters, then get down to this today. A chat to an older person could help you to put your mind in order and reinforce your belief in yourself.

WEDNESDAY, 16TH JUNE
Sun trine Mars

You may have too much energy for your own good today. This suggests that you will be champing at the bit, trying to get things done and full of good intentions. However, you also have a lingering desire to escape and to wander off into the land of dreams, and this strangely split mood of yours will make it difficult for you to achieve much.

THURSDAY, 17TH JUNE
Moon opposite Uranus

Take care today because there will be a sudden and unexpected setback to your

SCORPIO

plans. Guard against accidents at work or in the home. A friend may not fulfil his or her promises to you today and your family will be to ready to tell you that you have been taken for a fool. Maybe they are right, maybe not. You acted in good faith, however, and the laws of karma will put things right in the end.

FRIDAY, 18TH JUNE
Moon trine Jupiter

There is no doubt that you are on the way up the career ladder these days. A woman will be instrumental in helping you and there may be a golden financial opportunity in the offing that you shouldn't miss.

SATURDAY, 19TH JUNE
Venus square Saturn

You must try to use a measure of tact and diplomacy today in order to get what you want out of others. You may be tempted to remind of them of their duty or to point out all those things that they should have done but haven't, but this approach won't get you anywhere. Remember the old saying, it is far easier to catch flies with honey than with vinegar. (But who wants to catch flies anyway?)

SUNDAY, 20TH JUNE
Sun sextile Jupiter

Luck and opportunity are with you today. Those whom you are closely associated with will have good news about money and business matters now. So, if your fortunes are tied up with a particular firm or organization, an improvement in their prospects will also help you.

MONDAY, 21ST JUNE
Sun into Cancer

The Sun moves into your Solar ninth house today and it will stay there for a month. This would be a good time to travel overseas or to explore new neighbourhoods. It is also a good time to take up an interest in spiritual matters. You may find yourself keen to read about religious or philosophical subjects or even to explore the world of psychic healing over the next month or so.

TUESDAY, 22ND JUNE
Venus opposite Uranus

It's an ill wind that blows no one any good, and today's ill wind, though distressing for someone else may be just the opportunity that you have been looking for. The fall from grace of a colleague may be a stepping stone to achievement for you.

SCORPIO

WEDNESDAY, 23RD JUNE
Mercury square Mars

Be careful when operating machinery today, especially if you use any of this directly or indirectly for travelling purposes. Check any equipment that is mobile or portable before using it now, please. For instance, you may have an old faithful dual-voltage hairdryer that is just about to blow itself apart! Don't allow water anywhere near electrical appliances today (or any other day, for that matter!).

THURSDAY, 24TH JUNE
Moon opposite Saturn

Other people seem to be landing you with a number of unwanted problems these days, because they want you to shoulder their responsibilities for them rather than making the effort to do this for themselves. You may have to deal with a really awkward person today, perhaps one of those 'it's more than my job's worth' kind of officials. Whatever the problem, you will have to put your foot down in order to prevent yourself from being pushed around or used.

FRIDAY, 25TH JUNE
Mercury square Jupiter

You are full of great ideas and you would love others to be as inspired by them as you are. Unfortunately, today is not the day for this. Others will be keen to keep your nose to the grindstone and to give you the most boring chores to do.

SATURDAY, 26TH JUNE
Mercury into Leo

There's a certain flexibility entering your career structure as indicated by the presence of Mercury in your Solar area of ambition from today. You can now turn your acute mind to all sorts of career problems and solve them to everyone's satisfaction and your own personal advantage. Your powers of persuasion will be heightened from now on, ensuring that you charm bosses and employers to get your own way. Those seeking work should attend interviews because their personality will shine.

SUNDAY, 27TH JUNE
Moon trine Venus

Anything connected with your work, ambitions and financial fortunes should go very well indeed today. This is a happy, positive day so you'll be quite content with your lot at the moment. Perhaps you're developing a value system that really gives you inner satisfaction.

SCORPIO

MONDAY, 28TH JUNE
Jupiter into Taurus

You'll experience a deep need for companionship in the coming months as Jupiter moves into your Solar area of partnerships from today. Solitude is the last thing you want now and you will go to great lengths to make sure that you are never lonely.

TUESDAY, 29TH JUNE
Moon trine Saturn

This is a wonderful day for putting your ideas across to others. If you want to speak of how you feel or to make them understand what makes you tick, you will find just the right language in which to do this today.

WEDNESDAY, 30TH JUNE
Mercury opposite Neptune

This is not a day in which you should make far-reaching decisions either about your domestic arrangements or career matters. You won't be in the most logical frame of mind and you should leave such serious concerns to another day.

July at a Glance

LOVE	♥	♥	♥		
WORK	★	★	★	★	★
MONEY	£	£	£	£	
HEALTH	✛	✛			
LUCK	♘	♘	♘	♘	♘

THURSDAY, 1ST JULY
Moon sextile Pluto

Today is an excellent day to buy anything for the home. If you are married or in a settled partnership, then the two of you should look around the shops or scan the catalogues for anything that you want, because there are bargains to be found. You and your loved ones seem to be on the same wavelength just now and the atmosphere in your home should be pleasantly relaxed.

SCORPIO

FRIDAY, 2ND JULY
Moon opposite Venus

After an early frivolous mood, you may think that you can have too much of a good thing. It's not that you're back to earth with a bump, yet you're now keen to get back to more mundane pastimes and duties. It's time to catch up on neglected chores simply to take your mind off some sensitive issues in your life. Even you realize it's a good thing to have your feet on the ground.

SATURDAY, 3RD JULY
Moon trine Mars

You're filled to the brim with enthusiasm and vitality as the power of Mars courses through your chart. You're in the mood for fun and the energy of the fiery planet ensures that you are going to make the most of life today! Your creative interests, talents and sporting activities receive a welcome boost. You may even feel inclined to have a small gamble. You may not win much, but you'll certainly enjoy the flutter!

SUNDAY, 4TH JULY
Mars opposite Jupiter

Before you throw caution to the wind and wildly rejoice at some good news that comes your way, it would be wise to check out the facts first. You may have the wrong end of the stick and you'd only look silly if you allowed your exuberance to get the better of you.

MONDAY, 5TH JULY
Mars into Scorpio

Mars moves into your own sign enhancing your energy and drive. Your confidence takes a boost after a time of suppression and makes you more self-assertive than ever. The only thing to guard against is a tendency to be hasty, so try to slow down while driving or operating any machinery. This overall speedy feel to the planet makes minor accidents likely.

TUESDAY, 6TH JULY
Moon square Sun

You may find it hard to concentrate on your usual chores today because other things seem to be intruding on your mind. It would be nice just to sit and dream or to stand gazing out of the window for an hour or so, but the chances are that you won't be able to do any of this. Your mind is full of interesting philosophical thoughts and ideas but the work also needs to be done.

SCORPIO

WEDNESDAY, 7TH JULY
Moon trine Venus

Your job, career or business is taking precedence just at the moment. This is probably not the time to be terribly creative or experimental in what you are doing but simply to plod along your usual path and do what you have to do. You may have nothing more exciting than household chores to occupy yourself with now but these have to be done and you might as well do them properly.

THURSDAY, 8TH JULY
Mercury trine Pluto

If you are trying to raise money for a business venture or an enterprise of any kind, today should be a good day for this. You may have to take others into your confidence now, but the chances are that they will help you rather than take advantage of your openness.

FRIDAY, 9TH JULY
Moon square Venus

A woman may be a bit of a pain in the neck to you today and your relationships with women in general seem to be less than good. Partnerships of all kinds will need a bit of extra effort to make them work now and you may find that your other half is a bit downhearted or irritable now. It may be hard to influence those who matter or to make an impression on authority figures now.

SATURDAY, 10TH JULY
Moon sextile Mercury

Check out the rumours that are travelling around your workplace. There may be talk of mergers and takeovers and of hiring and firings. Some of these may only be rumours but other bits of information may have some truth in them. On a more personal level, this is a good time to get passionate with your partner and to enjoy your favourite and sexiest amusements.

SUNDAY, 11TH JULY
Mars square Neptune

There comes a time when you have to make a stand for your individual rights as opposed to those of your family. This is one of those times when a rebellious mood takes a hold. Any restriction on your actions will be met with hostility now!

MONDAY, 12TH JULY
Mercury retrograde

The fact that Mercury goes retrograde today throws a lot of your financial

SCORPIO

planning into confusion, and may even bring a note of embarrassment into a close relationship. There's obviously a topic which you feel impossible to approach now. At least this slow period will give you the chance to reassess both your sexual desires and the prospects of your financial fortunes. If things are going at a snail's pace now, you shouldn't be discouraged. It's for a good reason. One word of warning, don't enter any hire-purchase or other credit agreements until the middle of next month at the earliest.

TUESDAY, 13TH JULY
New Moon

The New Moon in your house of adventure urges you to push ahead with new projects. You're in a self-confident mood, and feel able to tackle anything the world throws at you. There's a lure of the exotic today as well, as far-off places exert a powerful attraction. Think again about widening your personal horizons, by travel or, indeed, by taking up an educational course. Intellectually you're on top form and your curiosity is boundless.

WEDNESDAY, 14TH JULY
Moon conjunct Mercury

Though the Lunar conjunction with Mercury is good news for your verbal self-expression you could easily get side-tracked by far more interesting things than work. You'll have a grasshopper mind now so it's very tempting to be more concerned with the doings of everyone else than getting your own head down. You know that you've got a lot on your plate so try to concentrate on the job in hand.

THURSDAY, 15TH JULY
Venus trine Jupiter

This should be a happy day because romantic Venus is in a good aspect to happy-go-lucky Jupiter today. You could fall crazily in love now, or you could rediscover the spark of romance in a current relationship. You or your partner could receive a windfall or an opportunity to do something really exciting. Travel plans are in the air and it may be that a friend offers you the chance of a trip.

FRIDAY, 16TH JULY
Mercury trine Pluto

Good news on the money front should occur today as Pluto makes contact with Mercury. Your ambitions too should take a step closer to fulfilment. A confidence given by a person of authority should be respected.

SCORPIO

SATURDAY, 17TH JULY
Void Moon

The Moon is 'void of course' today, so don't bother with anything important and don't start anything new now. Stick to your usual routines and don't change your lifestyle in any way.

SUNDAY, 18TH JULY
Saturn square Uranus

You will strongly wish to interfere in the life of someone close today. Although your motives are good ones, it will be hard to accept that everyone has their own decisions to make and you may have to put up with something that you disapprove of.

MONDAY, 19TH JULY
Moon trine Uranus

You can expect the unexpected in the domestic sphere of your life today. Friends may drop in unannounced and a family member may bring home a gift or a treat just for you. A loan may be repaid, and any favours that you have done to others may also be returned to you now. Your intuition will guide you strongly today and there may be some kind of inner voice which keeps you from saying or doing the wrong thing.

TUESDAY, 20TH JULY
Moon square Sun

It's a fairly mixed-up day emotionally speaking for you feel somewhat vulnerable and not your usual outgoing self at all. Though the trends are generally good, you can't quite believe your luck and will be waiting for something to go wrong. There may also be vague suspicion about a friend's motives but don't do anything about it just yet.

WEDNESDAY, 21ST JULY
Jupiter square Neptune

A new love in your life will not be approved of by members of your family. The same goes for any business partnership that is set up now. It's time to make a decision about where your loyalties actually lie.

THURSDAY, 22ND JULY
Mercury square Mars

Whatever you try to say today will seem to come out wrong. You may be so irritated by the behaviour of others that you lose your temper and thus lose your

SCORPIO

grip on the argument. It will be very hard for you to keep your cool because you want to move quickly and get things done fast today, while others are causing you delays and frustrations.

FRIDAY, 23RD JULY
Sun into Leo

The Sun moves decisively into your horoscope area of ambition from today bringing in an month when your worldly progress will achieve absolute priority. You need to feel that what you are doing is worthwhile and has more meaning than simply paying the bills. You may feel the urge to change you career, to make a long-term commitment to a worthwhile cause, or simply to demand recognition for past efforts. However this ambitious phase manifests, you can be sure that your prospects are considerably boosted from now on.

SATURDAY, 24TH JULY
Moon sextile Uranus

A family member could land you with some sort of unexpected expense today. However, this is not as bad as it seems because money will be coming in to replace the loss.

SUNDAY, 25TH JULY
Mercury square Jupiter

You will be at cross purposes with everyone around you today. You seem to be trying so hard to achieve a particular ambition, and other people seem to be dragging their feet and making it almost impossible for you to get anywhere. You need new faces around you and new contacts who might have the answers to your problems but it is hard to find the right people just now.

MONDAY, 26TH JULY
Sun opposite Neptune

It is hard for you to define your goals at the moment, let alone try to reach them. You may not know exactly what it is you want from life or you may find that your desires are changing in some kind of subtle way. For example, you may value freedom more than security just now, or you may think that it is better to help humanity in general rather than spend time doing nothing better than making loads of filthy money for yourself or your family! Don't worry, this crazy phase will pass and you will soon return to being greedy and acquisitive, just like the rest of us!

SCORPIO

TUESDAY, 27TH JULY
Sun square Jupiter

Someone may suggest that you get involved in their schemes today. If these schemes are small ones, they would merely cause you a modicum of irritation but if they are large ones, they could bring you real grief. Keep away from dodgy get-rich-quick ideas and stick to the job you know best. Don't allow others to persuade you that their ideas are a sure thing, because they aren't.

WEDNESDAY, 28TH JULY
Full Moon eclipse

Today's eclipse shows that you are at a critical period in your career. Of course the influence isn't specific to today, so for the next few weeks you'd be well advised to reassess your professional standing and direction. For many this eclipse is an astral message to abandon a job which no longer shows any sign of living up to your expectations. New ambitions will emerge and it's up to you to do something about them.

THURSDAY, 29TH JULY
Moon square Saturn

There may be tension in your home today and the chances are that this is being caused by the older members of the family. Your parents, in-laws, aunts, uncles and grandparents may be acting like a group of two-year-olds with indigestion today. You may be able to sort some of this out but if you can't, then go out and visit a friend's family instead!

FRIDAY, 30TH JULY
Sun trine Pluto

There's no doubt that today will provide a turning point for your career, your aspirations and your finances. This is all to the good as well. The splendid aspect between the Sun and Pluto encourages you to reach for the sky. You can do it, and you have the will and insight to make the most of any opportunity that comes your way.

SATURDAY, 31ST JULY
Mercury into retrograde

Mercury's return visit to your area of travel and learning shows that you can pick up a few tips that will be of use in the future. You may return to a country that you have previously visited within the next couple of weeks.

SCORPIO

August at a Glance

LOVE	♥	♥	♥	
WORK	★	★	★	★
MONEY	£	£	£	
HEALTH	✪	✪		
LUCK	♘	♘		

SUNDAY, 1ST AUGUST
Moon trine Mercury

It's an uplifting day as you see the possibilities of moving farther afield. Your adventurous outgoing mood is infectious now, and you'll find yourself the centre of romantic attraction. Your flirtatious attitude will find ready admirers. This is an excellent time to make travel plans and generally add to your social circle. There's amusement and interesting information to be gained from a child or younger person.

MONDAY, 2ND AUGUST
Moon trine Sun

The Moon is in excellent aspect to the Sun which both adds to your physical vitality and opens career opportunities. You could cope with anything now, and win through with ease. You're in tune with yourself. Your goals are clear and you'll be able to achieve them and still have time to spare.

TUESDAY, 3RD AUGUST
Venus trine Jupiter

This is bound to be a tremendously social day with lots of fun and good company to amuse you. Jupiter and Venus team up to provide jollity and a sense of belonging. You will be more optimistic and forward-thinking than you have been in ages.

WEDNESDAY, 4TH AUGUST
Moon trine Venus

Things are looking up now! Those of you who are alone and lonely would do well to get out and about today, because there is definitely something in the air. A

SCORPIO

friend may introduce you to a potential mate or you may make new friends now who may turn into lovers at a later date. Those of you who are happily settled will enjoy the company of your partner and also of good friends later on today.

THURSDAY, 5TH AUGUST
Moon conjunct Saturn

It looks as if, at long last, you are beginning to get things right in connection with relationships. There is still much work to be done and nothing is going to improve overnight. It is clear that more effort will have to be made. However, the outlook is much brighter and it looks as though any decisions that you take now will have an excellent long-term outlook.

FRIDAY, 6TH AUGUST
Mercury direct

The movement of Mercury into direct motion always brings periods of muddle and hesitation to a welcome end. If you have lost valuable bits of paper or misplaced your house keys, you can expect all these to be returned to you now. If your car has been off the road, it should be back on its wheels again and in fine fettle soon. If you have been vaguely fed up, your usual optimism will return.

SATURDAY, 7TH AUGUST
Sun square Mars

Before you get on your high horse, remind yourself that confrontation will harm your cause today. I know that you're irritated by hidebound convention and red tape, yet losing your temper won't win any co-operation or sympathy now. Subtle diplomacy is the key to progress, but I doubt whether you've got the patience or the inclination to try it out. Retire from the field of battle before you say too much and try again tomorrow.

SUNDAY, 8TH AUGUST
Sun opposite Uranus

There will be setbacks to your plans today and a number of things may go suddenly and inexplicably wrong. Murphy's Law is in operation now, so don't expect to get very far with anything at the moment. You may have to spend time mending or replacing things that have been accidentally broken or ruined. This is not a long-term trend but it can be the start of a frustrating few days.

MONDAY, 9TH AUGUST
Moon sextile Saturn

A dutiful visit to in-laws or elderly relatives is on the cards today. You may dread

SCORPIO

the prospect but it's not going to be half as bad as you think. In fact you could learn something to your advantage.

TUESDAY, 10TH AUGUST
Sun square Saturn

You know what your goals are but others may be keen to deflect you from your path or suggest that you follow a completely different course that suits their interests rather than yours. There is no need to lose your temper but a bit of gentle assertiveness will show these people that you mean business.

WEDNESDAY, 11TH AUGUST
New Moon eclipse

Although Nostradamus has predicted doom and disaster for today, Sasha and Jonathan are more optimistic. The stars are highlighting your direction in life which suggests that you need to think clearly, set goals and then go all out to reach them. Don't allow slower people to hold you back and don't allow those who are jealous or resentful of your success to put obstacles in your way. It seems to be most important that you forge ahead now while the going is so good.

THURSDAY, 12TH AUGUST
Mercury into Leo

Your job will take precedence today and you must make an effort to get your voice heard. Fortunately, this will not be too difficult because your superiors and your colleagues will be reasonably ready to hear what you have to say. You may have some bright ideas in other areas of life today as well, and you shouldn't hesitate to put these into practice.

FRIDAY, 13TH AUGUST
Mercury opposite Neptune

Work pressures seem to be heavy at the moment with you as the ready scapegoat for anything that goes wrong. Your family circle won't help much either since they seem so wrapped up in their own worries that they'll have little time for yours.

SATURDAY, 14TH AUGUST
Mars opposite Saturn

A too-ing and fro-ing sort of day with indecision ruling all affairs of the heart. All partnership issues are dodgy ground today so take care. This applies to business dealings as well as more personal partnerships.

SCORPIO

SUNDAY, 15TH AUGUST
Venus retrograde

Venus's return to your house of ambitions suggests that you have another chance to tie up loose ends and to finally achieve a goal that you have cherished. Women will be particularly helpful now.

MONDAY, 16TH AUGUST
Moon sextile Sun

Your mood is calm and you seem content to go along with what others want today. Fortunately, others seem to want much the same as you do, so there shouldn't be any conflict of interests now.

TUESDAY, 17TH AUGUST
Mercury square Jupiter

Discussing aims that are important to you will win little favour with your partner in life. It may be that your vision of the future is totally different from the one cherished by your spouse. Today's stars could point to underlying tensions in your relationship.

WEDNESDAY, 18TH AUGUST
Moon opposite Saturn

You will have to analyse the state of one of your relationships today. This may be an important one such as a marriage but it could be a friendship or a working relationship that needs to be thought through. You seem to be doing too much of the giving for too little in exchange and you will have to work out whether the situation warrants a change. You don't need to do anything drastic, but a few minor adjustments in terms of what you do for others are necessary.

THURSDAY, 19TH AUGUST
Pluto direct

After a long period of retrograde movement, Pluto now moves into direct motion. This is a distant and very slow-moving and very distant planet and its movements tend to go slowly and last a long time. For example, Mercury moves backwards three times a year for two to three weeks each time, while Pluto can spend a third of a year in retrograde motion. This forward movement in your Solar second house of money and possessions will make it easier for you to sort out or to improve your financial position from now on.

SCORPIO

FRIDAY, 20TH AUGUST
Sun conjunct Venus

A charming, diplomatic approach will work wonders in any employment dispute today. You can pour oil on troubled waters with very little effort and turn sworn enemies into allies. Women in the workplace will be very influential now. If you're seeking employment, you can be sure that your true qualities will shine through to any prospective boss.

SATURDAY, 21ST AUGUST
Moon trine Venus

You will be in a happy and loving mood today and this will lead you straight to the shops in order to buy your loved ones a gift or two. You won't be able to resist splashing out for them or for yourself now; however, anything that you buy now will turn out to be good value and probably great fun too. There is a loving feeling around you now but there is also a tinge of seriousness and of long-term planning in your mind now too.

SUNDAY, 22ND AUGUST
Moon trine Jupiter

Your home and domestic circumstances are really rather good today and whatever you have in mind will go particularly well. You may be keen to move house or to put your own home into some kind of new order and this is the time to get this into action. Your partner will have good news in connection with money or business matters and this too will help to ease any financial burdens in the home.

MONDAY, 23RD AUGUST
Sun into Virgo

As the Sun makes its yearly entrance into your eleventh Solar house, you can be sure that friends and acquaintances are going to have a powerful influence on your prospects. The Sun's harmonious angle to your own sign gives an optimism and vitality to your outgoing nature. Social life will increase in importance over the next month. You'll be a popular and much sought-after person. Obstacles that have irritated you will now be swept away.

TUESDAY, 24TH AUGUST
Venus square Mars

There seems to be something or somebody standing in the way of your progress today. However hard you work, trying to impress others with your diligence will be an uphill struggle for a while. This doesn't mean that you shouldn't make the

SCORPIO

effort, it is just that others will seem to have all the glamour, success and also the accolades that you would like. Fortunately, this trend is only temporary.

WEDNESDAY, 25TH AUGUST
Jupiter retrograde

Jupiter goes into retrograde motion for a while from today. Relationship matters may seem to grind to a halt now, so if you were thinking off popping the question or making some other long-term commitment, it would be best to wait for a better time. Nothing will be lost in this period, but you must accept that emotional affairs are going to drag at a snail's pace for a few months.

THURSDAY, 26TH AUGUST
Full Moon

Your creative soul and romantic yearnings come under the influence of today's Full Moon, so it's time to take stock of those things in your life that no longer give any emotional satisfaction. Children and younger people may need a word or two of advice now and the love lives of all around you will become the centre of interest. You're own romantic prospects may see an upturn too.

FRIDAY, 27TH AUGUST
Mercury conjunct Venus

Don't hide your light under a bushel today but set out to impress others with your knowledge and erudition. The image that you project is important to your progress now and your ability to charm those who matter will help you make the grade.

SATURDAY, 28TH AUGUST
Sun trine Jupiter

This could be a spectacularly good day in which you meet the love of your life! You could receive a totally unexpected windfall or you could have a terrific win if you are in the mood for gambling. Don't put your shirt on anything just because the planets are looking good, however; be sensible and you won't be disappointed if this doesn't work out. The outlook is good but it is hard to say just where your lucky break will come; it may not come from the direction that you most expect it to.

SUNDAY, 29TH AUGUST
Moon trine Pluto

You will find a way to successfully transform some element of your job into a form which suits you better in the future. You will also find a way of earning more money now, even though it may be a while before you see the results of all your efforts.

SCORPIO

MONDAY, 30TH AUGUST
Saturn retrograde

Saturn turns to retrograde motion today and it does so in your seventh Solar house of partnerships. This may slow down any plans you have to get together with your lover. If you are alone now, there is little chance of making new personal relationships while Saturn is in this retro-direction. Concentrate instead on work, your hobbies and on making friends for the time being.

TUESDAY, 31ST AUGUST
Mercury into Virgo

The swift-moving planet Mercury enters your eleventh Solar house today and gives a remarkable uplift to your social prospects. During the next few weeks you'll find yourself at the centre point of friendly interactions. People will seek you out for the pleasure of your company. It's also a good time to get in contact with distant friends and those you haven't seen for a while. The only fly in the ointment is that you shouldn't expect a small phone bill.

September at a Glance

LOVE	♥	♥	♥		
WORK	★	★	★	★	★
MONEY	£				
HEALTH	✪				
LUCK	♘	♘			

WEDNESDAY, 1ST SEPTEMBER
Moon square Venus

Today's stars could go two ways – either you are so wrapped up with your own schemes that you tend to neglect the one you love, or you'll be so wrapped up in a romantic atmosphere that you lose all sense of practicality. Keeping a sense of balance is of course the answer. Ensure that you get the boring stuff out of the way before you get to the loving togetherness.

SCORPIO

THURSDAY, 2ND SEPTEMBER
Mars into Sagittarius

Mars moves into your Solar house of finance and income from today and draws your attention to urgent matters that should have been dealt with long ago. If you've let your economic realities slide, then now's the time to rectify the situation before the expense becomes unbearable. You can focus an abundance of energy towards increasing your income now. Unnecessary expenditures will be reviewed and some much needed economies made. Swift action is your forte.

FRIDAY, 3RD SEPTEMBER
Mercury trine Jupiter

Everything that is offbeat and unusual will appeal to you today. New people and new interests are coming your way but they are very different from those who have surrounded you up till now. You seem to be looking for mental stimulation and the stars are ensuring that you will find what you need. You could take up a new interest or get into some kind of fascinating new study project now.

SATURDAY, 4TH SEPTEMBER
Mercury square Pluto

You may suffer from a short, sharp financial problem over the next couple of days or so. This is because you are being made aware that you need to think about your finances and to do something about them. It is no good being the last of the big spenders or you will soon be broke. Start to save something for a rainy day from now on.

SUNDAY, 5TH SEPTEMBER
Moon sextile Saturn

A serious talk with a partner will result in a renewed understanding and you may even benefit from advice given. This applies in both personal life and in business so be prepared to take another's views on board.

MONDAY, 6TH SEPTEMBER
Mars sextile Neptune

If you've been thinking of home improvement, or even of changing your abode entirely, then this is the day to start. You can turn your dreams into reality with just a little effort.

TUESDAY, 7TH SEPTEMBER
Moon opposite Uranus

It is hard to reconcile the needs of your job and of your family today. If you don't

SCORPIO

actually have a job, then it may be someone else's job that gets in the way. Alternatively, it is possible that someone else's lack of a job could be a sticking point. At any rate, you feel cramped and pressured both in and out of the home now.

WEDNESDAY, 8TH SEPTEMBER
Sun conjunct Mercury

The conjunction of the Sun and Mercury makes this one of the most exciting days of the year. Your mentality is on top from and communications of all kinds will work to your benefit. You can't let others make all the running now, get out and about, circulate. You'll find that friends, colleagues and supporters will all help you make your dreams come true. You have the heaven-sent ability to be in the right place at the right time and, more importantly, to say the right things!

THURSDAY, 9TH SEPTEMBER
New Moon

There's no doubt that issues surrounding friendship and trust are very important now. The New Moon in your horoscopic area of social activities ensures that encounters with interesting people will yield new and enduring friendships. Though your mood has tended to vary between optimism and despair recently, the New Moon can't fail to increase your confidence and vitality.

FRIDAY, 10TH SEPTEMBER
Sun trine Saturn

Other people will be amazingly helpful to you now. Friends will rush round to lend a hand and your lover will show you what he or she is all about by standing by you and giving you the help and encouragement that you need. Authority figures and father figures will also be amazingly good to you now and the advice that they give and example they set is worth following.

SATURDAY, 11TH SEPTEMBER
Venus direct

Venus's return to direct motion shows that you have nearly reached a cherished goal. An ambition that you once thought out of reach is obviously now within your grasp.

SUNDAY, 12TH SEPTEMBER
Moon sextile Venus

This is a good time to go out looking for gifts for others. You may have a reason for buying presents for others right now, but even if you don't we're sure you'll

SCORPIO

find an excuse. Take a look around and see if you can do a bit of early Christmas shopping so that you can save time, shoeleather and money later in the year. This is a good time to buy yourself a few small luxuries as well as buying them for others.

MONDAY, 13TH SEPTEMBER
Moon square Neptune

If your head feels as if it's stuffed with cotton wool, and you find yourself incapable of rational thought, we're not surprised! At least this vague influence won't last long!

TUESDAY, 14TH SEPTEMBER
Moon opposite Saturn

Love affairs and marital relationships are not always sweetness and light as we all know, but today's stars highlight the fact by putting one or both of you in such a stubborn mood that gloomy silence is set to reign for a while. Fortunately, this is nothing more than a passing phase and no serious damage will be done.

WEDNESDAY, 15TH SEPTEMBER
Mars conjunct Pluto

This is something of a turning point day in connection with your financial situation. You may decide to start a long-term savings scheme now or to open a joint account of some kind with another person. You may change the way you run a small business or you may just take some kind of financial advice. You will definitely get more control over your own purse strings from now on.

THURSDAY, 16TH SEPTEMBER
Mercury into Libra

You'll find yourself in a more introspective mood for a few weeks because Mercury, planet of the mind, enters the most secret and inward-looking portion of your horoscope from today. This is the start of a period when you'll want to understand the inner being, your own desires and motivations. Too much hectic life will prove a distraction now so go by instinct and seek out solitude when you feel like it.

FRIDAY, 17TH SEPTEMBER
Mercury trine Neptune

This is likely to be a strange and surprising day in which you will have some kind of unforgettable psychic or spooky experience. If you are asked to attend a seance, then do so! If you see a ghost, don't be surprised (or frightened for that

SCORPIO

matter). You may discover some kind of psychic or strange intuitive ability within yourself or you may find that a friend is involved in these kinds of things.

SATURDAY, 18TH SEPTEMBER
Moon square Mercury

Guard your tongue today because it's too easy to let your eloquence run away with you. You may find yourself betraying a confidence and that would do your reputation no good at all. Take care whom you talk to, and remember that walls have ears. Gossip you hear will be misleading and shouldn't be accepted as truth.

SUNDAY, 19TH SEPTEMBER
Moon trine Saturn

There aren't many problems that can't be solved if you take the time to sit down and discuss them sensibly with your other half. A problem shared is a problem halved.

MONDAY, 20TH SEPTEMBER
Moon trine Sun

Popularity is the keyword of the day and a cheery smile and a few moments spent in conversation will restore your perspective on life. You'll be sought out for the pleasure of your company. This is a lucky day, but don't bite off more than you can chew simply because everything's going so well. You'll end up with a mountain of unfinished duties… and it's a different story tomorrow.

TUESDAY, 21ST SEPTEMBER
Mercury sextile Pluto

You seem keen to maintain a low profile just at the moment and we consider that you are right to do so. It seems a good idea to keep any details of your current financial position to yourself at the moment too.

WEDNESDAY, 22ND SEPTEMBER
Moon opposite Venus

Today should be an active one around the home; the trouble is that you'd far rather be left to your own devices at the moment. Everywhere you turn you find another demand from a family member who won't be easily put off. Visitors too prove to be a distraction. You'll have to grin and bear it this once.

THURSDAY, 23RD SEPTEMBER
Sun into Libra

The Sun moves into your house of secrets and psychology today making you very

SCORPIO

aware of your own inner world of dreams and imagination. For the next month you'll be very aware of the hurdles that face you, and all those things that tend to restrict your freedom. However your imagination and almost psychic insight will provide the necessary clues to overcome these obstacles. Issues of privacy are very important for the next few weeks.

FRIDAY, 24TH SEPTEMBER
Mars sextile Uranus

Value for money is your first priority today. You're likely to have something spectacular in mind for your home and will bend heaven and earth to get your own way. At least you can be sure that whatever you spend on this project will be worthwhile.

SATURDAY, 25TH SEPTEMBER
Full Moon

Something is coming to a head in relation to your job. This is not a major crisis and there is absolutely no need to flounce out of a perfectly good job, but there is a problem that should be solved before you can continue on in a happy and peaceful frame of mind. You may have to sort out what your role is and which part of the job other people should be doing, because it looks as if you are carrying too much of the load at the moment.

SUNDAY, 26TH SEPTEMBER
Moon opposite Mercury

We suppose that it's excusable (just) but some of the words of flattery are just too fanciful to be true. We know that you're not averse to ardent declarations but you really should keep your tongue in your cheek and not be taken in by the charmers you'll meet today. On the other hand, if you've been feeling insecure this should be a boost to your ego.

MONDAY, 27TH SEPTEMBER
Moon square Neptune

Your imagination is likely to run riot today. You may convince yourself that your partner has a string of lovers or that your family are doing all kinds of nasty things behind your back. This kind of paranoia affects everyone from time to time, so just ignore it.

TUESDAY, 28TH SEPTEMBER
Moon conjunct Saturn

You may find yourself very attracted to someone older and more sophisticated.

SCORPIO

It is easy to see how a woman can be drawn to a powerful and charismatic man but the same goes for men these days. So, male readers can find themselves being drawn to a highly intelligent and competent female executive.

WEDNESDAY, 29TH SEPTEMBER
Moon trine Neptune

Sensitive areas can be tackled with ease under the rays of the Moon and Neptune. Family issues which have been troublesome can now be solved since you are so sensitive to the feelings of those around you.

THURSDAY, 30TH SEPTEMBER
Moon trine Uranus

You may come up with a sensible way of increasing the value of your home today, and this may set you off on a course of building or decorating. The same goes for any other land or property that you own. Any ideas of this kind could come from an acquaintance or from some other kind of unusual outside source. Talk any ideas over with your partner to see whether he or she agrees with them.

October at a Glance

LOVE	♥	♥	♥		
WORK	★	★	★	★	★
MONEY	£	£	£	£	£
HEALTH	✪	✪	✪	✪	✪
LUCK	♘				

FRIDAY, 1ST OCTOBER
Sun sextile Pluto

You seem to be on an inward journey today. Maybe you need to work out what your true values are and how they match up with those of the people who are around you. If there is a choice between doing something dishonest for short-term gains or doing without the goodies in order to remain honest, decent and true to yourself, you know you will make the right decision.

SCORPIO

SATURDAY, 2ND OCTOBER
Mercury sextile Venus

A woman will help you to sort out your priorities today and to begin to crystallize your goals and ambitions for the year ahead. You won't have all the answers yet, but a good chat with this most sensible of friends or colleagues will go a long way towards clearing your head. You may enjoy a visit to some kind of cultural, artistic or musical event later in the day.

SUNDAY, 3RD OCTOBER
Moon square Mercury

You could be having some kind of crisis of conscience today because you are finding it hard to go along with the beliefs or the behaviour of others. If others insist on breaking the law or on behaving in a particularly spiteful or nasty manner to a third party, then keep yourself right out of the situation and do what you know to be right. Keep to the straight and narrow and you can't go wrong.

MONDAY, 4TH OCTOBER
Moon sextile Sun

If you want a job done properly you'll have to do it yourself today. This is no great hardship since you'll actually enjoy what you are doing as long as you are left in peace to get on with it.

TUESDAY, 5TH OCTOBER
Mercury into Scorpio

The movement of Mercury into your own sign signals the start of a period of much clearer thinking for you. You will know where you want to go and what you want to do from now on. It will be quite easy for you to influence others with the brilliance of your ideas and you will also be able to project just the right image. Guard against trying to crowd too much into one day today.

WEDNESDAY, 6TH OCTOBER
Sun trine Uranus

A sudden and unexpected windfall could come your way today. However, this is unlikely to be in the form of cash because it is much more likely to be in the form of a bargain for the home. You may find just the piece of furniture you are looking for advertised on the notice board in your local supermarket. You may find a bike for the kids, or possibly a useful tool or a gardening implement at just the right price.

SCORPIO

THURSDAY, 7TH OCTOBER
Venus into Virgo

Venus moves into your eleventh house of friendship and group activities today, bringing a few weeks of happiness and harmony for you and your friends. You could fall in love under this transit or you could reaffirm your feelings towards a current partner. You should be looking and feeling rather good now but, if not, this is a good time to spend some money on your appearance and also to do something about any nagging health problems.

FRIDAY, 8TH OCTOBER
Moon trine Neptune

You need some peace and quiet so rest up and take it easy in the tranquillity of your own space. Allow yourself at least some time today to just sit there and do not much at all.

SATURDAY, 9TH OCTOBER
New Moon

The world of romance is especially attractive on a day when your dreams and fantasies take over your life. The New Moon points the way to new emotional experiences in the future, but you mustn't cling to the past because of misplaced loyalty or guilt. Some people are leaving your life, but if you were honest you'd admit that they're no real loss. Follow your instincts now and your dreams may well come true.

SUNDAY, 10TH OCTOBER
Venus trine Jupiter

This should be a day notable for fun, conviviality and plenty of laughs. Those two merry planets, Jupiter and Venus, team up to provide you and your friends the time of your lives. Go with the flow and enjoy it!

MONDAY, 11TH OCTOBER
Jupiter square Neptune

Your partner may go into an inexplicable sulk today. There's not much that you can do about this except wait patiently for the mood to break. Forcing the issue will not solve anything and may even make it worse. You can bet that there's a difficult family issue behind this!

TUESDAY, 12TH OCTOBER
Void Moon

This is not a great day in which to decide anything or to start anything new. A

SCORPIO

void Moon suggests that there are no major planetary aspects being made, either between planets or involving the Sun or the Moon. This is a fairly unusual situation but it does happen from time to time and the only way to deal with it is to stick to your usual routines and do nothing special for a while.

WEDNESDAY, 13TH OCTOBER
Mercury square Uranus

You could be a little too blunt for comfort today since you won't be able to see any earthly reason why you should keep your opinions to yourself, no matter how controversial they might be!

THURSDAY, 14TH OCTOBER
Neptune direct

The large and distant planet, Neptune, turns to direct motion today, thereby ending a period of muddle and confusion in the domestic and family area of your life. If it has been hard to understand the motives and actions of some family members, then all will be revealed. Once you know what is behind their recent strange behaviour, it will be much easier to cope with it.

FRIDAY, 15TH OCTOBER
Moon conjunct Mar

You've got the energy and drive to make the most out of your cash flow today. The Lunar conjunction with Mars in the most financially aware area of your chart helps you to overcome any monetary crisis. A sudden boost to your income could come through a job or investment opportunity. As with all Mars aspects, this one too warns against acting on impulse.

SATURDAY, 16TH OCTOBER
Mercury opposite Saturn

You may find yourself disagreeing with a partner over who does what. A more subtle form of competitiveness may emerge where someone tries to undermine your position or tries to show you up in front of others. You may do the right thing but at the wrong time or in the wrong way, and others may be pressuring you to point where you can't fit in all that you need to do.

SUNDAY, 17TH OCTOBER
Mars into Capricorn

Mars marches into your communications house today, so being direct, not to say forceful in speech will be a feature of the next few weeks. If you've got something to say, then there's no power in heaven or earth that's going to prevent you from

SCORPIO

saying it! If talking to a friend or relative has been like walking on eggshells, you'll make it clear that you aren't going to pussyfoot around sensitive topics any more! Be prepared for some heated words to clear the air!

MONDAY, 18TH OCTOBER
Venus square Pluto

Though your desires are inclined to extravagant fun, the financial realities won't permit you to spend, spend, spend. A female friend who could be a bad influence could leave your life at this time.

TUESDAY, 19TH OCTOBER
Moon square Saturn

Your mood will not be on top form as the Moon contacts grim Saturn. The most minor domestic or relationship upset could send you into a pit of gloom. Resist this negative outlook as much as you can.

WEDNESDAY, 20TH OCTOBER
Moon sextile Jupiter

This is a great day to spend time with your lover. A feeling of togetherness is obvious, add to this some soft lights and music and you have the perfect recipe for romance. A perfect gesture of affection will set your hearts aglow.

THURSDAY, 21ST OCTOBER
Moon opposite Venus

Your energy level is low at the moment, so don't set yourself a list of tiresome tasks. Just go through the motions while at work. Plan an evening of resting on the sofa, watching your favourite video or chatting idly to your lover. Don't put any demands upon yourself today, get a 'take-away' dinner (a 'carry-out' to all our American readers!), and read the papers until you doze off.

FRIDAY, 22ND OCTOBER
Sun square Neptune

This is likely to be a muddled and difficult day. Something could come back from your past in order to haunt you or to cause you embarrassment. For example, you may have forgotten to do something or you may have done something in a sloppy or inefficient manner simply in order to save time or to cut corners, and this problem may now reveal itself in an inconvenient manner.

SCORPIO

SATURDAY, 23RD OCTOBER
Sun into Scorpio

The Sun moves into your own sign today bringing with it a lifting of your spirits and a gaining of confidence all round. Your birthday will soon be here and we hope that it will be a good one for you. You may see more of your family than is usual now and there should be some socializing and partying to look forward to. Music belongs to the realm of the Sun, so treat yourself to a musical treat soon.

SUNDAY, 24TH OCTOBER
Full Moon

The Full Moon shines in the area of close relationships today. Since it is a stress indicator, you'd be wise to build some bridges within a close partnership now, either that or be content to let an emotional link drift... possibly away! Your understanding and tolerance will be the key to relationship success now.

MONDAY, 25TH OCTOBER
Venus trine Saturn

Your feelings run high today. Venus and Saturn combine to suddenly overturn previously strong inhibitions and to encourage you to express your deep feeling forcefully and with passion. A sudden infatuation could sweep you off your feet now.

TUESDAY, 26TH OCTOBER
Moon opposite Mercury

'Love don't come easy', as the song says. Well, not today, anyhow. It is not worth trying to get on good terms with your lover today, because everything you try to say or do will be misconstrued. Your motives may be the best but your partner will not be in the best of moods and he or she may be more interested in having a fit of the sulks than in giving you the love and reassurance that you are searching for.

WEDNESDAY, 27TH OCTOBER
Moon opposite Pluto

Guard against being manipulated by others or of agreeing to anything that you are responsible for when you are not in possession of the full facts. Be on guard against those who want to manipulate you for their own ends either in connection with money or with a relationship matter.

THURSDAY, 28TH OCTOBER
Mercury sextile Neptune

If you are looking for inspiration, you should find it quite easily now. The same thing applies to anything that requires the ability to think clearly and concisely. You

SCORPIO

are on top form today and can achieve anything you want. Your family is on your side and even your love life is falling nicely into place.

FRIDAY, 29TH OCTOBER
Moon opposite Mars

If you plan to travel today, you will face sudden setbacks and delays. If you use any kind of equipment for purposes of communication, this could also let you down. This means that the phone could go on the blink, as could your word processor, your fax or anything else that you rely on. The same goes for any kind of vehicle that you depend upon.

SATURDAY, 30TH OCTOBER
Mercury into Sagittarius

All the planets seem to be restless just now since Mercury changes sign today. At least you can get your mind into gear concerning the state of your finances now. Tasks you've been putting off like cancelling useless standing orders or ensuring you receive the most advantageous interest from your savings will be tackled with ease now.

SUNDAY, 31ST OCTOBER
Moon square Sun

There could be some kind of power struggle going on today. In practical terms, this could bring you up against an authority figure or someone who thinks rather a lot of themselves. This could also make things difficult for any business dealings that you have on the go at the moment. However, on a less practical note, you may doubt your own judgement for a while.

November at a Glance

LOVE	♥				
WORK	★	★	★	★	
MONEY	£	£	£		
HEALTH	☉	☉	☉	☉	☉
LUCK	♘	♘	♘	♘	♘

SCORPIO

MONDAY, 1ST NOVEMBER
Void Moon

Today is one of those odd days when there are no important planetary aspects being made, not even to the Moon. The best way to tackle these kinds of days is to stick to your usual routine and to avoid starting anything new or tackling anything of major importance. If you do decide to do something large today, then it will take longer and be harder to cope with than it would normally.

TUESDAY, 2ND NOVEMBER
Moon square Mercury

A friend may tell you something that upsets you today while another friend may do something that costs you money. With friends like these, do you really need enemies? Your mind is not working at its best now so don't agree to anything or do anything that you are unhappy about or unsure about. Wait until your judgement is working at full strength once again.

WEDNESDAY, 3RD NOVEMBER
Moon trine Saturn

An older relative or someone who is in a position of authority could be of considerable help to you today. You and your partner may have to work your way through a number of official or governmental regulations and this older or wiser person could be just the one to help you.

THURSDAY, 4TH NOVEMBER
Moon sextile Mercury

Keep a few matters to yourself today. Even if a friend or a neighbour tries to worm things out of you, try to keep your mouth firmly shut. Your financial position is improving rapidly now but it would be a good idea to keep this information to yourself just at the moment because there are plenty of people around you who would be only too happy to relieve you of any extra pennies that you may have put by.

FRIDAY, 5TH NOVEMBER
Moon trine Uranus

A friend could help you sort out a difficult task, especially if this is related to your home or your family in some way. You may hear about family secrets that have been kept dark for years, or perhaps some kind of other family news may come to your ears now. If a family member has been ill or in hospital, there will be good news about them today.

SCORPIO

SATURDAY, 6TH NOVEMBER
Sun opposite Saturn

Just when you thought everything was going swimmingly, there seems to be a spanner being thrown into the works! A partner, a lover or a close working associate could mess things up for you in a complete and utter manner. On the other hand, you may be blithely going up an altogether wrong road until someone close to you points out just how misguided you are being.

SUNDAY, 7TH NOVEMBER
Sun sextile Mars

It's a very good day for all sorts of intellectual interests. You need some mental challenge to get your brain racing, and today's stars give you the opportunity to do just that. Established routines won't hold much appeal for you need variety. Short journeys, even if it's only down to a local store will stimulate your mind. You may meet an old friend who will be buzzing with news and gossip. More seriously, you could consider taking up an educational course to satisfy your curiosity on any subject that takes your fancy.

MONDAY, 8TH NOVEMBER
New Moon

There's a New Moon in your own sign. This is a powerfully positive influence that encourages you to make a new start. Personal opportunities are about to change your life. You must now be prepared to leave the past behind to embark on a brand new course. Decide what you want, because you'll be your own best guide now.

TUESDAY, 9TH NOVEMBER
Mercury into Scorpio

It seems to be the time for major planetary movements for Mercury races into your own sign now, giving you not only an eloquent tongue, but the opportunity to express your ideas and inspirations clearly and persuasively. You have a busy period coming up with constant letters and phone calls bringing gossip, laughs and fascinating information your way.

WEDNESDAY, 10TH NOVEMBER
Moon sextile Uranus

A family member could receive a small windfall today. Even if this stroke of luck doesn't come in the form of money, it will be something that both you and they will appreciate and value.

SCORPIO

THURSDAY, 11TH NOVEMBER
Moon trine Jupiter

Today's stars show a windfall for many. It may not be much, but it's enough to disturb your ordered routine with a burst of excitement. Money gains aside, the good it will do to your frame of mind is the best feature of the day. Treat yourself to something nice in the way of a celebration.

FRIDAY, 12TH NOVEMBER
Moon square Venus

You may want to laze the day away doing nothing more than doze in a deckchair, snoozing and reading your favourite magazine. Unfortunately, this is unlikely to be the way the day works out. Just when you thought you had done all the chores, someone will ring and ask you to start afresh.

SATURDAY, 13TH NOVEMBER
Moon conjunct Mars

There could be some interesting events in connection with brothers and sisters today. They may spring a pleasant surprise on you or they may have good news of their own to impart. Neighbours too could have cheery things to tell you and all these characters will be very helpful to you if you need them to give you a hand. Any mechanical problems that have been bothering you will be easily solved today.

SUNDAY, 14TH NOVEMBER
Saturn square Uranus

Trying to mediate in a dispute between your partner and the rest of the family will be a thankless task, but one that you seem honour bound to undertake today! The contrasting forces of Uranus and Saturn tend to put you in a no-win situation!

MONDAY, 15TH NOVEMBER
Moon square Saturn

Someone close is weighed down by worry and lack of self-esteem at the moment. Though you are sympathetic, the best plan is to do something practical to increase this person's confidence rather than just being a sounding post.

TUESDAY, 16TH NOVEMBER
Mercury sextile Mars

The pen is mightier than the sword they say, and that's certainly true for you today! However, you may extend the quote to include the tongue as well since you'll be forthright, logical and verbally devastating if anyone should dare to oppose you!

SCORPIO

WEDNESDAY, 17TH NOVEMBER
Venus sextile Pluto

Dreams of romance could be turned into concrete reality with a bit of help from lady luck today. Take the opportunity to talk to that person whom you fancy so much and see whether you receive a reply that is worth hearing.

THURSDAY, 18TH NOVEMBER
Moon trine Mercury

This looks like being rather a good day for you, so enjoy yourself. You should be filled with bright ideas today which you are simply raring to put into practice. If, despite all this brilliance, you are still missing a vital piece of information, try asking around among the members of your family or among your neighbours.

FRIDAY, 19TH NOVEMBER
Moon sextile Neptune

You'll be in a businesslike mood today. That's not to say that your mind will be on the job though. Any routine work can be accomplished with ease, but the reason for that is that you'll be thinking happy thoughts and dreaming about the future. Nothing wrong in that, just so long as your tasks get done.

SATURDAY, 20TH NOVEMBER
Venus trine Uranus

You seem to have a stroke of genius today that helps you either to get a creative project onto the right lines or to sort out some kind of domestic dispute, or both. A woman will be very helpful, possibly coming up with just the right idea at the right moment. Home is where the heart is today, so stay close to the kitchen and the hearth with your lover and keep the rest of the world at a distance.

SUNDAY, 21ST NOVEMBER
Mars square Jupiter

Tempers are gong to run high today. The Martial aspect to Jupiter makes you very defensive and likely to over-react to any criticism of your work – whether it's intended or not! You're also inclined to dramatize everything and cast yourself in the leading role as the wounded hero. Pull yourself together, and don't rise to the bait every time!

MONDAY, 22ND NOVEMBER
Sun into Sagittarius

Your financial prospects take an upturn from today as the Sun enters your house of money and possessions. The next month should see an improvement in your economic security. It may be that you need to lay plans to ensure maximum profit now. Don't expect any swift returns from investments but lay down a pattern for future growth. Sensible monetary decisions made now will pay off in a big way.

TUESDAY, 23RD NOVEMBER
Full Moon

The Full Moon brings to the surface intense feelings that you have buried away in some vault of memory. You'll be forced to look at yourself stripped bare of illusions now. That's not such a bad things because you'll realize that many of your hang-ups have been a total waste of time and should be ditched. You may have a financial worry coming to a head so today's Full Moon encourages you to take decisive action to sort it out once and for all.

WEDNESDAY, 24TH NOVEMBER
Moon trine Venus

Your imagination is very powerful today, and your thoughts will turn to the romantic and erotic issues of your life again and again. It's said that dreams are quite often more fun than fact and that's certainly true of your mood today. This can't be bad for your sex life since your imagination can only provide some spice to your relationship.

THURSDAY, 25TH NOVEMBER
Sun sextile Neptune

It would be a good idea to stay close to home today and to indulge yourself by dabbling in your favourite hobbies and interests. Photography, dressmaking or any other kind of craft or creative interest would go well today. Get out into the garden if you can or do something to make your home attractive or to replace bits and pieces that have got tatty.

FRIDAY, 26TH NOVEMBER
Mars into Aquarius

Your energies will be directed to your home and the area around it. Thus you may spend time working on or in the home or on the land around the place today. If the dishes are piling up in the kitchen, then get down to washing them up and if you haven't a clean shirt or a pair of socks to match, then get around to doing the washing now. Mars in the domestic area of your life over the next few weeks could bring a rash of plumbers, builders and all kinds of other domestic workmen your way.

SCORPIO

SATURDAY, 27TH NOVEMBER
Moon opposite Neptune

This is not a day to anything too strenuous, and certainly it's not one for making any long-term decisions. It won't be much use looking to your family or colleagues for guidance either because they'll be as confused as you are!

SUNDAY, 28TH NOVEMBER
Moon square Mercury

The pressures of life are sometimes too much even for you to bear. Your thoughts are clouded by the Moon and Mercury now so you're in need of an ego boost to offset the criticism and lack of appreciation you've found recently in the workplace. We all need our dreams, so indulge yourself in something you really like, and never mind what anyone else thinks of it.

MONDAY, 29TH NOVEMBER
Mars conjunct Neptune

You have every intention of getting on with a number of jobs in the home today but something seems to be getting in the way of your progress. Just as you start to work, your eye is caught by a newspaper article or an item on the television and, guess what? You immediately stop what you are doing.

TUESDAY, 30TH NOVEMBER
Moon trine Saturn

You know where you are going and what you want from life and, fortunately for you, your partners, associates and even your lover are completely in tune with your needs at this time.

December at a Glance

LOVE	♥	♥	♥	♥	♥
WORK	★	★	★		
MONEY	£	£	£	£	
HEALTH	✪	✪	✪	✪	
LUCK	♘	♘	♘	♘	♘

SCORPIO

WEDNESDAY, 1ST DECEMBER
Venus opposite Jupiter

Try not to make any extravagant claims today. Boasting could cost your dear since there's always someone who will want you to prove your claims. It's not wise to overestimate your abilities either. You may think that you can take the world on and win, but when it comes down to practicalities you'll have to admit that you can't do everything on your own. Don't let a desire to please prompt you into making promises you can't keep.

THURSDAY, 2ND DECEMBER
Moon sextile Sun

Money may be the root of all evil but it's worse still not having any! It is obvious that you are doing a lot of thinking about the state of your finances and, more importantly, the things of true value in your life today.

FRIDAY, 3RD DECEMBER
Moon opposite Jupiter

We think that you're rather tired today. It's possible that you've been taking on too much just to show how impressive you can be. Are you sure that you're not playing the martyr and going for the sympathy vote? It doesn't really matter because the fact remains that you could do with a quiet undemanding day, so make sure you get one.

SATURDAY, 4TH DECEMBER
Moon square Neptune

You'll have a problem concentrating on anything today because the Lunar aspect to Neptune makes your attention span very short indeed. You could be rather vague too so be prepared for some puzzled looks from your family.

SUNDAY, 5TH DECEMBER
Venus into Scorpio

The luxury-loving planet, Venus, is suggesting that this is a great time to spoil yourself and also to enjoy yourself. So treat yourself to something nice and new that is for you alone. A new outfit would be a good idea or a few nice-smelling toiletries. Throw a party for your favourite friends and don't look the other way if someone seems to be fancying you.

MONDAY, 6TH DECEMBER
Sun sextile Uranus

A kind of breakthrough could occur today. This may be a stroke of genius on your

SCORPIO

behalf or a really cracking idea that is put to you by a friend. The outcome could be an opportunity to increase your funds. If you are looking for a new place to live, you could stumble across the just the right thing today and, what is more, this could happen in the most bizarre manner.

TUESDAY, 7TH DECEMBER
New Moon

Today's New Moon shows that your financial affairs have reached a point where you have to make a decision. Do you carry on in the old and rather dreary ways of making and spending your cash or will you look at the realities and make sensible decisions? This isn't a time to retreat into dreamland, or to carry on with bad budgeting. Look at your monetary state carefully now.

WEDNESDAY, 8TH DECEMBER
Venus square Neptune

Don't take too much on trust today because nothing is quite what it seems to be. If a casual friend cries on your shoulder, then be sympathetic by all means, but try to avoid taking their problems on your back if you can.

THURSDAY, 9TH DECEMBER
Moon sextile Venus

You're particularly charming and seductive today. You could use your wiles to get your own way in anything, as there are few with enough mental resistance to turn you down flat! You'll be at the centre of attraction. Affection will be shown to you and you'll be left in no doubt that all around you regard you with fondness and respect.

FRIDAY, 10TH DECEMBER
Mars square Saturn

Domestic conflict seems certain today as those two difficult planets, Mars and Saturn, team up to spread disruption and discord through your home and family. Try to keep calm and refuse to rise to the bait.

SATURDAY, 11TH DECEMBER
Mercury into Sagittarius

Mercury's timely entry into your financial sector should be a great help to your situation. Your mind will now be clear and you can see all issues from a logical standpoint. Now you'll be able to budget sensibly, pay off outstanding debts and generally make sense of your cash flow. The shrewdness that Mercury brings to bear on your economic life will enable you to control income and expenditure.

SCORPIO

SUNDAY, 12TH DECEMBER
Mercury sextile Neptune

The value of money is a lesson we all must learn at some time, and the sooner the better. You are well equipped to teach it to a spendthrift relative now and can get through to the most obstinate of people!

MONDAY, 13TH DECEMBER
Moon sextile Sun

Home life and comfort move to centre stage today as the Moon makes a positive aspect to the Sun. All those luxuries that you crave may come a step nearer today, as you realize that you can afford to treat yourself. Perhaps some new furniture is in the offing.

TUESDAY, 14TH DECEMBER
Mars conjunct Uranus

Harsh words and rebellious attitudes are to be expected in your family circle today. The conjunction of aggressive Mars with unpredictable Uranus could open a can of worms which will be difficult to handle. It may not actually be serious, but it will certainly be loud.

WEDNESDAY, 15TH DECEMBER
Venus opposite Saturn

There is no doubt that something serious is happening to your love life. You may be forming a new and important partnership now or, alternatively, bringing something that has become boring and irritating to a complete end. Even if you are ending a friendship or partnership of some description, this only leaves the door open for a new one to creep in.

THURSDAY, 16TH DECEMBER
Moon sextile Neptune

Routine housework and daily domestic duties will prove to be more comforting in their sameness than otherwise today. You could tackle anything at the moment simply because you'll be content in your own surroundings.

FRIDAY, 17TH DECEMBER
Sun trine Jupiter

You know that you are right and that your thinking is just about spot on today. Fortunately for you, other people also know that you are right too and are not about to give you any kind of unwelcome arguments today.

SCORPIO

SATURDAY, 18TH DECEMBER
Mercury conjunct Pluto

Don't allow others to talk you into doing something that you really feel is wrong for you. If you can avoid lending anything today, then do so. On the other hand, guard against manipulating others for your own ends now. If something needs to be changed, you have the courage to do it now.

SUNDAY, 19TH DECEMBER
Moon conjunct Saturn

Your other half or a close friend is likely to be rather depressed today. You'll have to be very understanding and show a lot of sympathy. However, a practical attitude to solving problems will be more helpful in the long run.

MONDAY, 20TH DECEMBER
Jupiter into Aries

Jupiter's entry into your house of health and habits may not be good news for those prone to nervous tension but will improve your relations with colleagues, workmates and bosses. You'll find that all around you are prepared to drop their tasks in order to help you out.

TUESDAY, 21ST DECEMBER
Moon opposite Pluto

Take care not to be robbed or swindled today. Guard your wallet, purse, bag, pocket book or anything else that contains money, credit cards or other easily portable forms of funds. If you have a petty cash box, lock it and keep it out of sight. If you are working, then take only what you need for the day's spending and even then keep it in a locked drawer or out of sight.

WEDNESDAY, 22ND DECEMBER
Sun into Capricorn

Your curiosity will be massively stimulated from today as the Sun enters the area of learning and communication. Other people's business suddenly becomes your own now. That's not to say that you turn into a busybody overnight, it's just that many will turn to you for some guidance. Affairs in the lives of your brothers, sisters and neighbours have extra importance now. Short journeys too are well starred for one month.

THURSDAY, 23RD DECEMBER
Full Moon

Today's Full Moon brings a chance to banish confusion concerning your beliefs and

SCORPIO

value systems. You've become aware of certain contradictions and erroneous assumptions so it's high time that you thought these through and developed some watertight conclusions. Perhaps you've found that many of the concepts you learned in school are no longer relevant, so do something about it and express your own individuality.

FRIDAY, 24TH DECEMBER
Venus square Mars

Keep your mind on what you are doing in and around the home today. Mars is badly aspected and this could bring silly accidents while working around the place. It is a poor day for getting on with home improvements, decorating, dressmaking or fancy cooking. It would be better either to go out and get on with jobs elsewhere or simply to relax and forget the chores for once. It is Christmas Eve after all!.

SATURDAY, 25TH DECEMBER
Moon trine Pluto

Even though it's Christmas Day it is not a good time to be open about your plans but rather to go about things slowly and quietly until the time comes to speak out. Luck is with you in connection with money now too, and something that has been held up in the works may come through now. Merry Christmas!

SUNDAY, 26TH DECEMBER
Mercury sextile Mars

If you are searching for someone who shares your values and priorities, then today's excellent aspect between Mercury and Mars will help you to find just the right person. This doesn't necessarily mean that you will find the love of your life today, but you may discover a soulmate or a similar type of person to yourself among working colleagues or in your local neighbourhood.

MONDAY, 27TH DECEMBER
Mercury trine Jupiter

Though the planets do not necessarily indicate a change of job you might just receive a raise for the one that you are doing. For those seeking employment, Jupiter and Mercury ensure a successful outcome to their quest.

TUESDAY, 28TH DECEMBER
Moon square Mercury

Though you are a sociable sort of person, sometimes your friends are more of a pain than a pleasure. You are in a serious frame of mind just now and can't stand

SCORPIO

being pestered by frivolous people. They may have more than their share of seasonal spirit but for today at least, you seem quite immune. If you want to avoid irritation, pretend to be out.

WEDNESDAY, 29TH DECEMBER
Moon square Sun

Though you tend to be in a rather introspective mood today, too much preoccupation with your own thoughts and anxieties could result in you being left out by those who think you're nothing but a boring stick-in-the-mud. If you can tear yourself from your own fascinating thoughts a moment, you might meet someone who will interest and stimulate you far more.

THURSDAY, 30TH DECEMBER
Mars sextile Jupiter

You seem to be in the mood to make something of an effort today and this may manifest itself in a frenzied bout of work or by putting on the most impressive dinner party you can manage. You may have to put yourself out on behalf of your parents or other older family members today, which means that you may spend the day feeding or chauffeuring them all over the place.

FRIDAY, 31ST DECEMBER
Venus into Sagittarius

Your financial state should experience a welcome boost just in time for the new year as Venus, one of the planetary indicators of wealth, moves into your Solar house of possessions and economic security from today. You feel that you deserve a lifestyle full of luxury now and that'll be reflected in the good taste you express when making purchases for your home. Your sense of self-worth is boosted too, which might indicate a renewed interest in high fashion. Happy New Century!